Sundressing

Sundressing

Sew 21 Easy, Breezy Dresses
for Women and Girls

Melissa Mora

Fons&Porter

CINCINNATI, OHIO

contents

Introduction   6

1 Getting Started   8
These tools, techniques and measurement guides will help you make a dress that fits just right.

2 Everyday   24
Whether your day is busy or leisurely, these lovely dresses will get you a second look wherever you go.

3 City Chic   52
Take it downtown in stylish designs that perfectly marry wearability and fashion.

4 Al Fresco   84
The call of the great outdoors is easy to answer in pretty dresses that move with you.

5 Soiree   116
These showstoppers are so special that you'll want to wear them long after the party's over.

About the Author   156

Index   159

Introduction

I am a summer girl. Give me sunshine, a beach or a lawn, a field to pick flowers in, a dirt road to ride down. These are the settings of my happiest memories.

Sundressing is an attitude as much as a fashion statement for a season. It is the art of carrying sunshine on cold and cloudy days, of being at ease in your own skin. And in this book, I want to help you create both a summer wardrobe that can be enjoyed beyond the season, and an ease in your own skin.

Ease in my own skin did not come naturally to me. One of the seminal events of my childhood was moving from the city to the country, transferring to a small school where I was the outsider on many levels—unable to fit into any of the stereotypical slots reserved for students. My mom had always sewn, and so my clothes didn't fit the stereotypes either, but instead were created more and more in my own vision, especially as my sewing skills grew to match my mother's. In the pressure cooker of a small town filled with gossip, clothes were a way to purposely set myself apart.

It was only later, in high school, that participation in theater let me start to come into my own. Playing other people paradoxically made it easier to find and inhabit myself. It helped that I was also doing costume design at this point, wrestling with questions of how outer appearance reflects the inner self. And isn't that what getting dressed each day is all about? Which version of you do you want to be today?

The other facet of ease in one's own skin and clothing is the experience of today's fashion culture. The media bombard us with images of who we can be. Even when we find clothing that resonates with us, the experience of shopping and fitting into that clothing leaves a lot to be desired for anyone who doesn't have model measurements. That reason, above all others, is why I sew and why you should as well—short of bespoke couture (which is out of reach for my pocketbook!), the best way to feel good about yourself in clothing is to have clothing that fits your exact body. So this book also contains advice on fitting, to help you adapt the included patterns to your unique shape and to those of others if you are sewing for someone else.

Sundressing is a sensibility played out at barbecues and on vacations and in days without a plan. It's the slip dress you pull over a swimsuit at the pool and the frock you layer over leggings and under a sweater while dreaming of warmer days. It's the background for the bouquet of wildflowers spontaneously gifted. And it's the effortless style this book will help you create for yourself and the young ladies in your life.

How to use this book

It can be tempting, if you are an experienced sewist, to skip the sewing instructions at the front of the book and go straight to the patterns. I'd advise you not to do that in this case, as this book and the patterns included are a little different.

My aim with this book is to give you the tools to make your own unique and custom-fitted dresses. You will also find many charming designs for girls of all ages, from toddlers to preteens. (Incidentally, all of the dress names are inspired by the sights and sounds of Austin, my home city.)

The patterns are basic bodice blocks (on the sheet provided) and you are meant to fit them to yourself (or the wearer) in muslin form first. The "Getting Started" chapter explains how to get a perfect, customized fit. If you do this step first as intended, you should have minimal to no fitting to do for any of the dresses in the book.

After you have an altered pattern that fits perfectly, use that as the basis for each of the dresses in the book. Each dress will start with instructions to trace your front and back bodice. Trace off your altered and fitted pattern; then using the new copy, follow the instructions

for further alteration. You may want to make a muslin with your newly altered pattern to check that you like things such as the neckline or length, but generally if you fitted your original bodice pattern, things such as fit on the bust have already been done.

Each dress also has instructions for the skirt shown in the picture for that style. But don't be afraid to mix it up! Change the skirt length or style, try different fabrics and prints—make each dress truly a reflection of your (or the wearer's) personal style. Just know that the yardages given assume you will be sewing the entire dress, including linings, out of the same fabric. If you choose to change anything—say, you want to use different fabrics for the outside and the lining—make sure to recalculate your yardage.

I hope you enjoy unleashing your own creativity on these designs.

Happy sewing . . .

1

Getting Started

One of the keys to any creative endeavor, including sewing, is to use the right tools and techniques to get the end result you want. Whether you're gathering a skirt or installing a zipper, the right tools will make your life easier and help your finished garment to look polished and professional. Read on to review the tools and techniques used to make these dresses.

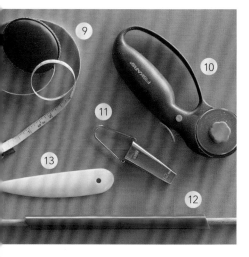
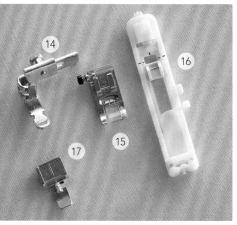

Tools and Materials

Anyone who sets out to sew is going to need some tools besides the sewing machine. Here's an overview of what you need and what might be nice to have.

The basics

1. Dressmaking shears
2. Straight pins
3. Seam ripper
4. Thread

These are the must-haves. Without them, you're not going to get far.

Marking tools

5. Tracing wheel
6. Tracing paper
7. Two-sided fabric marker
8. Chalk pen

A tracing wheel and tracing paper are my preferred method for transferring dart markings. You can also cut the darts out of the pattern and then trace the edges with a fabric marker or chalk pen.

Other tools

9. Measuring tape
10. Rotary cutting tool
11. Bias tape maker
12. Tube turner
13. Point turner

Straight lines are easier to cut with a rotary cutter and ruler. The measuring tape will help you get the most accurate fit. If you want more bias tape choices than what is available in a package, use a bias tape maker. The tube turner makes short work of thin shoulder straps, and the point turner helps you

get sharp corners without poking through your fabric.

Presser feet

14. Piping foot
15. Zigzag foot
16. Buttonhole foot
17. Zipper foot

A piping foot can also be used to install zippers. The zigzag sewing foot is the most often used. The buttonhole foot is useful for perfect buttonholes if your machine has an automatic buttonhole function. The standard zipper foot is used for sewing on zippers.

Fabrics

All kinds of lightweight to medium fabrics are suitable for sundressing. Keep in mind the feel and drape of the fabric—stiffer fabrics in a skirt will stand out from the body more, and fabrics with more drape will cling.

Some suggested fabrics are cotton and cotton blends, silk, voile, lawn, satin and taffeta.

You may also wish to add body to your dress bodice with interfacing. If so, choose an interfacing that matches the weight of your fabric.

Notions

Some of the dresses may call for lace, elastic or zippers. In general, I look for braided or knit elastic for a softer feel, and nylon coil zippers for ease of use. With lace, make sure to pay attention to care instructions for washing.

Sewing Techniques

The following techniques are used in dresses throughout the book. Refer back to this section when you come across something you're not sure how to do. And even if you're experienced at sewing, you may pick up a tip you haven't seen before.

How to install a zipper

Zippers don't have to be scary if you follow these tips and go slowly. If you prefer not to use the shortcut of tape to hold the zipper, you can also pin or baste.

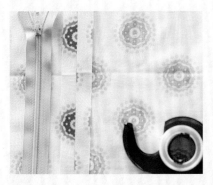

1 On the garment seam where the zipper will be inserted, mark the zipper end point as indicated in the specific pattern. With right sides together, baste the seam from the top of the pattern pieces to the marked point. Backstitch and finish stitching the seam with a regular stitch length. Press the seam open.

2 Place the zipper facedown on the seam, aligning the zipper coil with the seam line. Make sure to position the top of the zipper so that you account for the given seam allowance at the top of the garment.

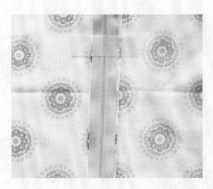

3 Use a few pieces of transparent tape to hold the zipper in place.

4 On the right side of the fabric, and using a zipper foot, stitch the zipper in place close to the seam line on each side.

5 Remove the transparent tape from the zipper.

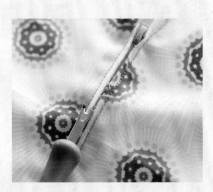

6 Use a seam ripper to remove the basting stitches holding the seam closed over the zipper.

How to gather fabric

Many of the dress projects feature gathered skirts. Keep in mind fabric weight for this technique—lighter weight fabrics gather more easily and add the least amount of bulk at the seam.

Stitch two lines of basting stitches within the seam allowance of the edge to be gathered, leaving long thread tails. Pull the bobbin thread tails to gather the fabric along the basting stitches, distributing gathers evenly over the width of the piece.

How to shirr with elastic thread

Another way to gather is by shirring with elastic thread. This technique works well on quilting weight or thinner fabrics, but not heavier fabrics such as twill gabardine.

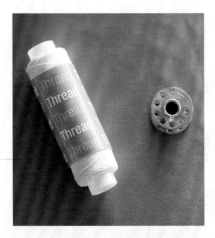

1 Begin by winding your bobbin with elastic thread. For drop-in bobbin type machines, I get best results by machine-winding the bobbin. With side-loading bobbins, handwinding the elastic thread seems to work best. You may need to play with both methods before finding which one works best with your machine.

2 Load the elastic bobbin and thread the needle with regular thread. Lengthen your stitches to 4–5mm. Sew several rows of stitches about ⅛" (3mm) apart.

3 For even more gathering, steam the back side of the stitching with a steam iron.

How to finish a seam

There are many options for seam finishes. The simplest is to trim the seam allowances with pinking shears. This works best with woven fabrics of natural fibers. Other options include overlocked seams, French seams and flat felled seams.

Overlocked seams

An overlocked seam is created with a special sewing machine (called a serger) or special stitch on a regular sewing machine. This stitch loops around the raw edge of the fabric, keeping it from fraying. You can also create a faux overlock stitch by sewing a wide stitch width, medium stitch length zigzag on the edge of your fabric and setting the needle to just miss the raw edge of your fabric on one side of the stitch.

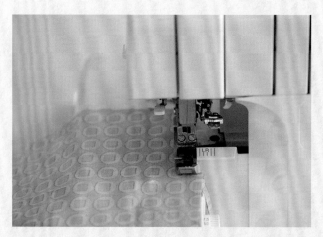

After stitching the seam on a regular sewing machine, sew the seam again in the serger, which has a knife that cuts the edge of the fabric while looping threads around the edge to prevent unraveling.

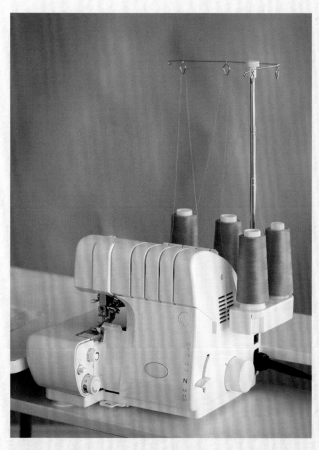

Some regular sewing machines have an overlock stitch, but the most common way to do an overlock seam finish is with a serger.

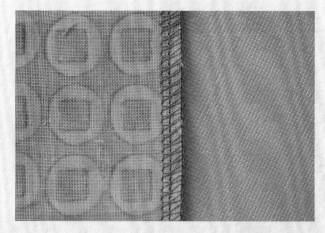

Finished overlocked seam

French seams

French seams enclose raw edges in a tube and work well on straight seams in non-bulky fabrics.

1 To sew a French seam that incorporates a ½" (1.3cm) seam allowance, start with the fabric wrong sides together. Sew the seam with a scant ⅛" (3mm) seam allowance.

2 Press the seam open, then fold the garment right sides together and press flat along the seam. Sew the seam again from the wrong side with a ⅜" (1cm) seam allowance, enclosing the seam and raw edges from the previous step inside.

Flat felled seams

Flat felled seams enclose raw edges by using a line of topstitching. This technique creates a slightly raised seam with a line of stitching on the right side, much like the seams on your jeans. This works well for bulky fabrics where decorative topstitching adds visual interest.

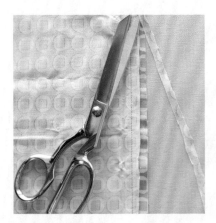

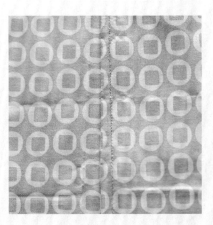

1 Stitch the seam right sides together, then trim one seam allowance to ¼" (6mm).

2 Press the raw edge of the longer seam allowance around and over the other seam allowance.

3 Press both seam allowances to one side and stitch the folded edge, encasing raw edges inside.

How to slipstitch by hand

The slipstitch, also known as a ladder stitch or blind stitch, is useful when you want to hide your stitching as much as possible. Use a single strand of thread in a color that matches the fabric for the most invisible look.

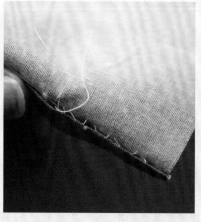

1 Begin with a single strand of thread, knotted at the end. Draw the needle and thread up through the fold of the hem or seam allowance.

2 Push the needle for a stitch along the fold line or in the seam allowance. Next, take a small horizontal stitch through the fabric on the opposite side.

3 Repeating the stitches from step 2 will create a "ladder" of parallel stitches. Pull the thread until the stitching lies flat and almost invisible. Remember to knot the thread before cutting it.

How to make a rolled hem

This technique creates a very narrow hem that is well suited to sheer fabrics. Rolled hems can also be created with a serger if you have one; see your machine manual for instructions.

1 Turn under the hem ¼"–½" (6mm–1.3cm) and press all around. Using an edge joining foot, stitch around the hem a scant ⅛" (3mm) from the fold.

2 Trim the raw edge as close to that stitch line as possible, being careful not to clip through the stitching.

3 Press under the tiny stitch hem and topstitch all the way around close to the fold.

Getting the Perfect Fit

We are going to make a dress that perfectly fits the wearer, and in order to do that we'll need to know the following measurements.

Adult measurements

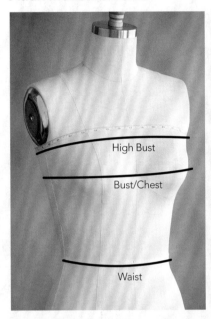

Child measurements

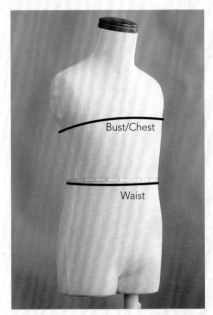

MEASUREMENTS FOR WOMEN	
High Bust	
Bust/Chest	
Waist	
Neck to Waist	

MEASUREMENTS FOR GIRLS	
Bust/Chest	
Waist	
Neck to Waist	

Tips for measuring

The bust or chest is measured around the fullest part, keeping the measuring tape level all around. Don't pull the tape tightly, but there shouldn't be slack either.

The high bust is measured under the arms and above the fullest part of the bust. The measuring tape will not be level.

The waist is measured where the indent in your side happens if you bend to the side. It's between the bottom of the rib cage and the belly button, which is not typically the level at which you wear your pants (unless you're rocking the high-waisted look). The measuring tape should be level.

DRESS MEASUREMENT GUIDE FOR WOMEN

Dress Size	High Bust	Bust/Chest	Waist	Neck to Waist
0	31" (78.7cm)	32" (81.3cm)	26" (66cm)	14½" (36.8cm)
2	32" (81.3cm)	33" (83.8cm)	27" (68.6cm)	15" (38.1cm)
4	33" (83.8cm)	34" (86.4cm)	28" (71.1cm)	15¼" (38.7cm)
6	34" (86.4cm)	35" (88.9cm)	29" (73.7cm)	15½" (39.4cm)
8	35" (88.9cm)	36" (91.4cm)	30" (76.2cm)	15¾" (40cm)
10	36" (91.4cm)	37" (94cm)	31" (78.7cm)	16" (40.6cm)
12	37" (94cm)	38" (96.5cm)	32" (81.3cm)	16¼" (41.3cm)
14	39" (99.1cm)	40" (101.6cm)	34" (86.4cm)	16½" (41.9cm)
16	40" (101.6cm)	42" (106.7cm)	36" (91.4cm)	16¾" (42.5cm)
18	42" (106.7cm)	44" (111.8cm)	38" (96.5cm)	17" (43.2cm)
20	43" (109.2cm)	46" (116.8cm)	40" (101.6cm)	17¼" (43.8cm)
22	45" (114.3cm)	48" (121.9cm)	42" (106.7cm)	17½" (44.5cm)

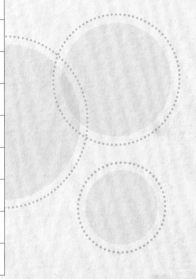

DRESS MEASUREMENT GUIDE FOR GIRLS

Dress Size	Bust/Chest	Waist	Neck to Waist
2T	20" (50.8cm)	19" (48.3cm)	9" (22.9cm)
3T	21" (53.3cm)	20" (50.8cm)	9½" (24.1cm)
4T	22" (55.9cm)	21" (53.3cm)	10" (25.4cm)
5	23" (58.4cm)	22" (55.9cm)	10½" (26.7cm)
6	24" (61cm)	23" (58.4cm)	11" (27.9cm)
8	26" (66cm)	24" (61cm)	12" (30.5cm)
10	28" (71.1cm)	25" (63.5cm)	13" (33cm)
12	30" (76.2cm)	26" (66cm)	14" (35.6cm)

The waist to neck is measured vertically from the large vertebra at the base of the neck in the back to the level of the waist. It can help to tie a string or wear a belt at waist level to get an accurate measurement here.

If your measurements don't fall in line with one particular dress size on the measurement guide charts, first remember that sizes are just a starting point. The great thing about sewing is that you customize the fit for your own unique and beautiful body—or that of whomever is going to wear the dress you sew. Follow these guidelines to choose your starting size:

* **For girls:** Go with the bigger of the waist or bust/chest size.

* **For women:** If the high bust and waist measurements fall within the same dress size, go with that size. If they do not, go with the larger of the two to choose your starting size. A full bust or small bust adjustment will need to be done to alter the bodice so that the bust will fit perfectly.

Trace front and back bodice pattern pieces in your size from the bodice block sheet provided with the book. A tracing is best to work with (instead of cutting the pattern paper) so the sizing can be customized. Make sure to transfer the pattern markings to your tracing.

Fitting and making adjustments to a bodice pattern

First, let's adjust for length. If your neck to waist measurement differs from the measurement listed for the dress size chosen from the chart, you'll need to lengthen or shorten the bodice. Cut the tracing on the "Lengthen/Shorten" line. For a longer bodice, spread the pattern apart the length you need, add paper into the gap, and tape. For a shorter bodice, overlap the pattern pieces and tape. Blend the side seam.

Next, let's deal with full bust and small bust adjustments. If your high bust measurement puts you in a smaller starting size than your bust measurement, you'll need to do a full bust adjustment. If it puts you in a larger size, you'll need to do a small bust adjustment.

Note: Do not overlook the back bodice. It will require fewer adjustments, but you don't want to insert a zipper only to find that you should have adjusted down the center back or side seams. You should be able to address any back alterations at the muslin stage.

To adjust the bust (Figure 1)

Full bust and small bust adjustments start the same:

1. Draw a line to extend the center line of the waist dart straight up toward the shoulder.

2. Draw a line from the bust point to the square mark on the armhole curve.

3. Draw a line connecting the center line of the bust dart with the bust point.

4. Cut on the center line of the waist dart up to the bust point, then continue on the line toward the armhole. Do not cut all the way through the armhole, just close enough to create a hinge in the pattern that allows you to move the dart without changing the length of the armhole.

5. Cut through the center line of the bust dart almost to the bust point, creating another hinge in the pattern. Now, proceed to step 6 for making either a full bust or a small bust measurement.

For a full bust adjustment (Figure 2)

6. Using the pattern hinge from the armhole, move the side seam out until you have made the gap at bust point level equal to half the required extra bust width. For example, if your bust measurement is 2" (5.1cm) larger than the base size, you want the gap to be 1" (2.6cm) here. Add paper under the gap and tape this gap down.

7. Move the bust dart hinge so that the side seam is straight again. This will make the left side of the pattern longer than the center front of the pattern. Add paper under the bust dart and tape.

8. Add paper to the center front of the pattern so that the waist line is once again level.

9. Redraw the bust point at the same level as it was before the adjustment, in the center of the added paper.

10. Measure ½" (1.3cm) away from the bust point, lining your ruler up with the center of the bust dart. For each additional inch beyond 1 (2.6cm) that you spread the gap, measure another ½" (1.3cm) away from the bust point. For example, if you added a 2" (5.1cm) adjustment, measure ½" + ½" = 1" (1.3cm + 1.3cm = 2.6cm) away from the bust point. This is where your new bust dart will end. Make a mark, then connect this mark to the original dart legs at the side seams. Measure your dart legs and make sure they are the same length. If they are not, adjust your dart point up or down to make the legs the same length.

11. Redraw the waist dart so that it still ends at the same level, centered between the ends of the dart legs. It should point directly at your new bust point.

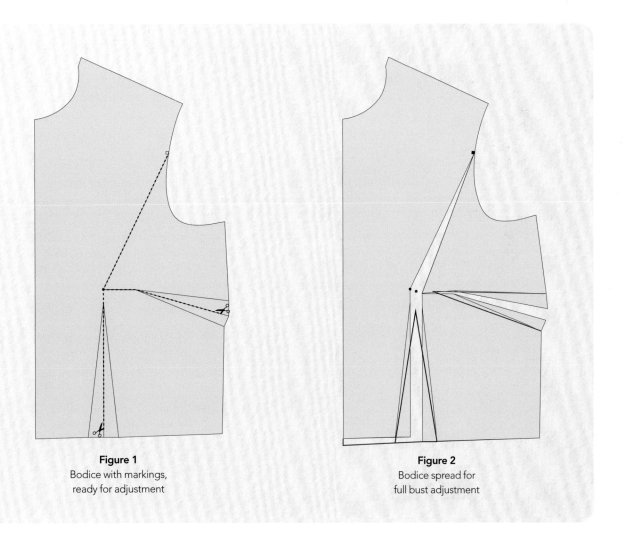

Figure 1
Bodice with markings,
ready for adjustment

Figure 2
Bodice spread for
full bust adjustment

For a small bust adjustment (Figure 3)

6. Using the pattern hinge from the armhole, move the side seam in until you have overlapped the pattern at bust point level equal to half the required less bust width. For example, if your bust measurement is 1" (2.6cm) less than the base size, you want to overlap ½" (1.3cm) here. Tape the pattern.

7. Move the bust dart hinge so that the side seam is straight again. This will make the left side of the pattern shorter than the center front of the pattern.

8. Cut the pattern at the center front so that the waist line is once again level.

9. Redraw the bust point at the same level as it was before the adjustment, using the line drawn up toward the shoulder as a guide to center it.

10. Measure ½" (1.3cm) away from the bust point, lining your ruler up with the center of the bust dart. This is where your new bust dart will end. Make a mark, then connect this mark to the original dart legs at the side seams. Measure your dart legs and make sure they are the same length. If they are not, adjust your dart point up or down to make the legs the same length.

11. Redraw the waist dart so that it still ends at the same level and points directly at your new bust point.

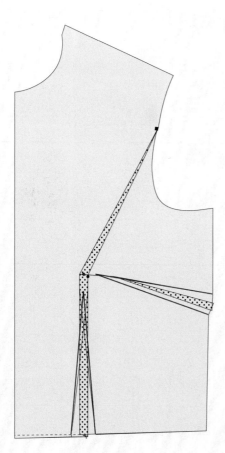

Figure 3
Bodice overlapped for
small bust adjustment

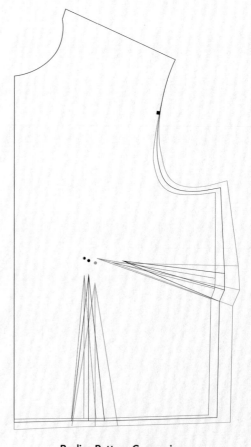

Bodice Pattern Comparison
Black = As drafted
Green = Adjusted for full bust
Orange = Adjusted for small bust

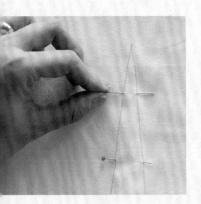

Checking your adjusted pattern

Once you are done adjusting the pattern, use it to cut out a muslin. Muslins are used to check fit before sewing a pattern. You can use muslin or any other inexpensive fabric to do this.

Sew the fit bodice using ½" (1.3cm) seam allowances and a basting stitch length.

1. Mark the darts on the muslin.

2. Pin and sew the darts (shown in photos), making sure to sew from the edge toward the point of each dart. Sew one stitch off the fabric at the point and leave long threads. Tie the threads together in a knot at the point of the dart. Press the bust darts down and the waist darts toward the side seams.

3. Sew the shoulder seams.

4. Sew the side seams.

Pin the bodice on by pinning the center back seam closed and check for fit. A properly fitted bodice should end at the natural waistline, and fit closely at the neck, waist, bust and armhole. There should be no gaping in the armhole area, and darts should point to the fullest part of the bust without encroaching all the way onto the bust. The waist dart should end just a bit below the fullest part of your bust, and the side dart should extend right down the middle of the side of your bust; not too high and not too low. Adjust the darts on your muslin as necessary to get the perfect fit. You can retrace them higher or lower, closer or farther away from center front as needed. If the waist dart is pinching too much, you can make it narrower; for gaping at the waist, increase the width of the dart.

Add any changes from the fit bodice to your pattern. You may wish to pull the basting threads out of your muslin to add the changes to your paper tracing. You may want to trace a clean copy at this point, as this perfectly fitting bodice will be the starting point for all the dresses you make for this wearer in the book.

When fitting, Make sure the armscye (armhole) fits snugly without gaping. Darts should point toward the apex of the bust, and stop short of the flat part at the front of the bust. The waist should fit snugly and at the natural waistline.

Skirts

Most of the dresses shown in this book have a gathered skirt, and a circle skirt is another option. The instructions will tell you which type appears in each project, but feel free to switch up the skirts for different looks.

Gathered skirts

Gathered skirts are rectangles that are gathered in at the waist. They tend to fall in small gathers down the length of the skirt, with some bulk at the waist (depending on how much the skirt is gathered). To make a gathered skirt, cut a rectangle of fabric that is 1.5 to 2 times as wide as the waist measurement for the size you are sewing. Make sure this measurement is bigger than the wearer's hip measurement and adjust if necessary. Determine the length of the skirt from the measurement guide charts that follow. For longer skirts in larger sizes, you may need to cut panels and seam them together to get a rectangle that is the right size.

Circle skirts

Circle skirts, in contrast, are more full around the hem and fitted at the waist, causing them to fall in wide folds with little bulk at the waist. To make a circle skirt, add 1" (2.6cm) to the waist measurement then divide that number by 6.28. This is number A. For number B, add 1" (2.6cm) to the length you want the final skirt to be. Then use numbers A and B to draft one-quarter of a circle as shown (**Figure 1**). *Tip:* If you don't have drafting paper available, rolled gift wrap paper works well.

If you fold your fabric parallel to the selvage once and then fold it perpendicular to the selvage once, you can cut the full circle skirt out of one piece of fabric. If you are making a very long skirt, you may need to cut three pieces and seam them together to make your circle (one piece is half the circle for the front, then two one-quarter circle pieces for the back with a center back seam). If you do this, make sure to add seam allowances to the sides of the one-half and one-quarter circle pieces before cutting.

Gathered skirt　　　　Circle skirt

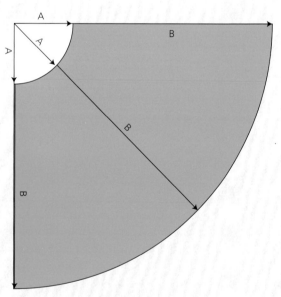

Figure 1
Using measurements A and B to draft
one-quarter of a circle skirt

SKIRT MEASUREMENT GUIDE FOR WOMEN
All measurements listed include the seam allowance and 1" (2.6cm) to hem.

Dress Size	Knee Length	Midi Length	Maxi Length
0	22½" (57.2cm)	30" (76.2cm)	37½" (95.3cm)
2	23" (58.4cm)	30½" (77.5cm)	38" (96.5cm)
4	23½" (59.7cm)	31" (78.7cm)	38½" (97.8cm)
6	24" (61cm)	31½" (80cm)	39" (99.1cm)
8	24½" (62.2cm)	32" (81.3cm)	39½" (100.3cm)
10	25" (63.5cm)	32½" (82.6cm)	40" (101.6cm)
12	25½" (64.8cm)	33" (83.8cm)	40½" (102.9cm)
14	26" (66cm)	33½" (85.1cm)	41" (104.1cm)
16	26½" (67.3cm)	34" (86.4cm)	41½" (105.4cm)
18	26¾" (67.9cm)	34¼" (87cm)	41¾" (106cm)
20	27" (68.6cm)	34½" (87.6cm)	42" (106.7cm)
22	27¼" (69.2cm)	34¾" (88.3cm)	42¼" (107.3cm)

SKIRT MEASUREMENT GUIDE FOR GIRLS
All measurements listed include the seam allowance and 1" (2.6cm) to hem.

Dress Size	Knee Length	Midi Length	Maxi Length
2T	12" (30.5cm)	16" (40.6cm)	20" (50.8cm)
3T	13" (33cm)	17" (43.2cm)	22" (55.9cm)
4T	15½" (39.4cm)	19½" (49.5cm)	24½" (62.2cm)
5	16½" (41.9cm)	21" (53.3cm)	25½" (64.8cm)
6	18" (45.7cm)	23" (58.4cm)	28" (71.1cm)
8	19" (48.3cm)	24½" (62.2cm)	30½" (77.5cm)
10	20" (50.8cm)	26½" (67.3cm)	33½" (85.1cm)
12	21" (53.3cm)	28" (71.1cm)	35½" (90.2cm)

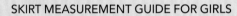

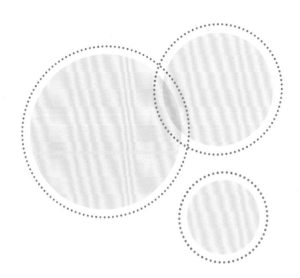

2

Everyday

Who needs pants?
With casual prints and breathable
fabrics such as cotton, you can look
more put together and stay cool in
these sundresses every day.

*P*rimrose dress

The simple lines of this classic sundress are the perfect backdrop for a gorgeous textile. Add embroidery to the skirt, showcase a special print or celebrate simplicity in a solid color of a sumptuous silk/cotton fabric.

Front

Back

Materials

FABRIC
Shown: 50-50 silk/cotton blend

Dress Size	44/45" (111.8/114.3cm)	or	58/60" (147.3/152.4cm)
0	2¾ yd (2.5m)		1⅓ yd (1.2m)
2	2¾ yd (2.5m)		1⅓ yd (1.2m)
4	2¾ yd (2.5m)		1⅓ yd (1.2m)
6	2¾ yd (2.5m)		1⅓ yd (1.2m)
8	2¾ yd (2.5m)		1⅓ yd (1.2m)
10	2¾ yd (2.5m)	or	2¾ yd (2.5m)
12	2¾ yd (2.5m)		2¾ yd (2.5m)
14	3¼ yd (3m)		2¾ yd (2.5m)
16	3¼ yd (3m)		2¾ yd (2.5m)
18	3¼ yd (3m)		2¾ yd (2.5m)
20	3¼ yd (3m)		2¾ yd (2.5m)
22	3¼ yd (3m)		2¾ yd (2.5m)

NOTIONS
14" (35.6cm) zipper

NOTES
Fabric amounts listed include enough for lining in the same fabric. Recalculate if using different material for lining.

½" (1.3cm) seams used unless otherwise noted.

Refer to Chapter 1 for basic sewing techniques and information on customizing fit.

Primrose Dress

1. Trace off the front and back bodice pieces.

2. Modify the front bodice.

   a. Make a mark on the neckline at about the halfway point of the curve. Draw a line (A) from here to the bust point (**Figure 1**).

   b. Cut through the center of the waist dart, to but not through the bust point (**Figure 2**).

   c. Cut the line from the neckline, to but not through the bust point (**Figure 2**).

   d. Rotate the top half of the bodice so that the neckline overlaps ½" (1.3cm). This will widen the waist dart (**Figure 2**).

   e. Make a mark on the center front 2¾" (7cm) down from the neckline edge. Draw a curved line (B) from this mark to the armhole for the new neckline (**Figure 3**).

   f. Cut the bodice along line B.

3. Modify the back bodice.

   a. Draw a 90° line (A) from the mark on the armhole of the back bodice to the center back (**Figure 4**).

   b. Extend the center line (B) of the waist dart straight up to touch line A (**Figure 5**).

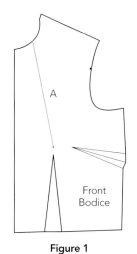

Front Bodice

Figure 1

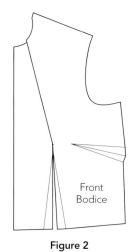

Front Bodice

Figure 2

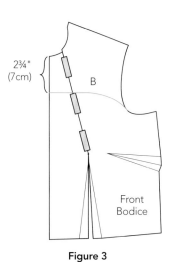

2¾" (7cm)

Front Bodice

Figure 3

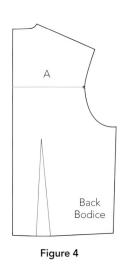

Back Bodice

Figure 4

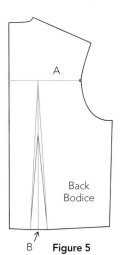

Back Bodice

Figure 5

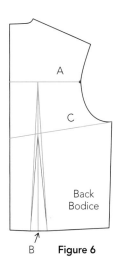

Back Bodice

Figure 6

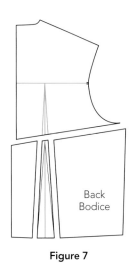

Back Bodice

Figure 7

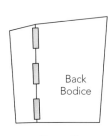

Back Bodice

Figure 8

c. Redraw the waist dart lines from the bottom of the dart legs to touch the point where line B touches line A (**Figure 5**).

d. Draw a line (C) from the bottom point of the armhole to the center back that touches the original top of the waist dart (**Figure 6**).

e. Cut the bodice pattern on line C and the new waist dart legs below line C (**Figure 7**).

f. Remove the dart piece and tape the remaining back bodice pieces together (**Figure 8**).

4. Cut one front bodice piece on the fold and cut two back bodice pieces (mirrored) out of outer fabric. Cut one front bodice piece on the fold and cut two back bodice pieces (mirrored) out of lining fabric. Mark the point where the back bodice pieces are taped together on the top edge; this is where the straps will attach.

5. Cut two straps 2" (5.1cm) wide by 18" (45.7cm) long.

6. For the skirt, cut a rectangle that is 2 times the waist measurement in width and knee length (see the skirt measurement guide in Chapter 1). If you need to cut panels of the skirt to get to the final rectangle size, cut one that is the waist measurement

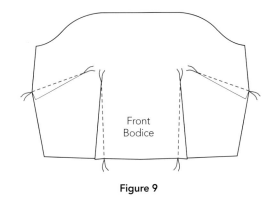

Figure 9

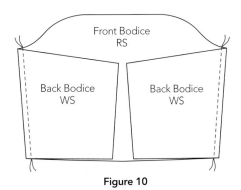

Figure 10

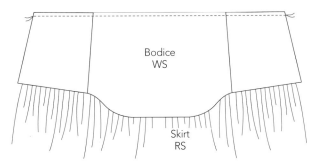

Figure 11

in width and two that are half that, then sew one shorter panel to each side of the longer panel. This way you will have side seams and a center back seam.

7. Sew the darts on the front bodice and lining (**Figure 9**).

8. Sew the two bodice back pieces to the bodice front along the side seams, right sides together. Repeat with the lining (**Figure 10**).

9. Finish the short raw edges of the skirt with an overlock stitch or faux overlock stitch.

10. Gather the top edge of the skirt to match the width of the bodice at the waistline.

11. Sew the bodice to the skirt along the waistline, right sides together (**Figure 11**). Press the waist-line seam toward the bodice.

12. Lay the zipper along one side of the center back of the dress and mark the bottom of the zipper.

13. Fold the dress right sides together, matching the center back edges. Baste the seam from the top edge to the zipper mark made, then backstitch and shorten to a regular stitch length for the rest of the seam. Press the seam open.

14. Insert the zipper in the center back seam (**Figure 12**).

15. Press the straps in half, wrong sides together, matching long edges. Open the straps. Press the raw edges toward the crease line, wrong sides together. Then press again on the original crease line. Your straps should now be ½" (1.3cm) wide. Topstitch down each side of the strap to finish.

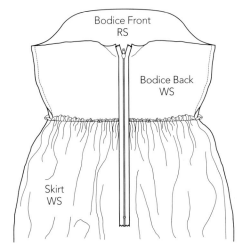

Figure 12

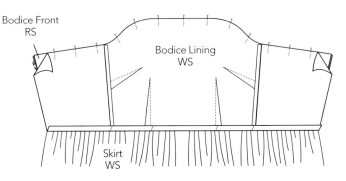

Figure 13

16. Pin the straps to the bodice front, directly above each waist dart point, with the straps pointing down. Baste in place.

17. Press the bottom edge of the lining ⅜" (1cm) to the wrong side.

18. Pin the bodice lining to the bodice along the neckline edge, right sides together. The lining should extend beyond the zipper ½" (1.3cm) on each side (Figure 13). Stitch the lining to the bodice, leaving ½" (1.3cm) wide openings at the strap marks on the bodice back.

19. Turn the lining to the inside of the dress. Press the neckline.

20. Turn the center back edges of the lining ½" (1.3cm) to the wrong side and pin, sandwiching the zipper between the lining and the outer fabric.

Stitch over the zipper line again, securing the lining, or hand-stitch to secure.

21. Pin the folded edge of the lining over the waistline seam (Figure 14).

22. On the right side of the dress, stitch in the ditch of the waistline seam to secure the lining (Figure 15).

23. Push the straps into the openings on the back bodice. Pin. Try the dress on and adjust the straps as needed. Topstitch the neckline edge of the dress, securing the back straps in the process.

24. Turn the bottom edge of the skirt ½" (1.3cm) to the wrong side twice and press to form a hem. Stitch the hem.

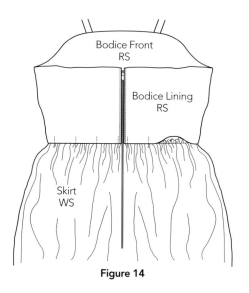

Figure 14

Figure 15

West Lynn dress

The long lines of this maxi dress and peekaboo skirt are both classic and sultry—the perfect summer mix. Whether you're dashing around town or picnicking in the park, this dress is a flawless choice when the temperatures rise.

Front

Back

Materials

FABRIC
Shown: Silk/cotton blend

Dress Size	44/45" (111.8/114.3cm)	or	58/60" (147.3/152.4cm)
0	3¾ yd (3.4m)		3¾ yd (3.4m)
2	3¾ yd (3.4m)		3¾ yd (3.4m)
4	3¾ yd (3.4m)		3¾ yd (3.4m)
6	3¾ yd (3.4m)		3¾ yd (3.4m)
8	3¾ yd (3.4m)		3¾ yd (3.4m)
10	3¾ yd (3.4m)		3¾ yd (3.4m)
12	3¾ yd (3.4m)	or	3¾ yd (3.4m)
14	5 yd (4.6m)		3¾ yd (3.4m)
16	5 yd (4.6m)		3¾ yd (3.4m)
18	5 yd (4.6m)		3¾ yd (3.4m)
20	5 yd (4.6m)		3¾ yd (3.4m)
22	5 yd (4.6m)		3¾ yd (3.4m)

NOTIONS
14" (35.6cm) zipper

1 yd of ⅜" (1cm) wide elastic

NOTES
Fabric amounts listed include enough for lining in the same fabric. Recalculate if using different material for lining.

½" (1.3cm) seams used unless otherwise noted.

Refer to Chapter 1 for basic sewing techniques and information on customizing fit.

West Lynn Dress

1. Trace off the front and back bodice pieces.

2. Modify the front bodice.

   a. Make a mark on the neckline at about the halfway point of the curve. Draw a line (A) from here to the bust point (**Figure 1**).

   b. Cut through the center of the waist dart, to but not through the bust point (**Figure 2**).

   c. Cut the line from the neckline, to but not through the bust point (**Figure 2**).

   d. Rotate the top half of the bodice so that the neckline overlaps ½" (1.3cm). This will widen the waist dart (**Figure 2**).

   e. Make a mark on the center front 2¾" (7cm) down from the neckline edge. Draw a curved line (B) from this mark to the armhole for the new neckline (**Figure 3**).

   f. Cut the bodice along line B.

3. Modify the back bodice.

   a. Draw a 90° line (A) from the mark on the armhole of the back bodice to the center back (**Figure 4**).

   b. Extend the center line (B) of the waist dart straight up to touch line A (**Figure 5**).

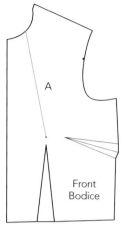

Figure 1

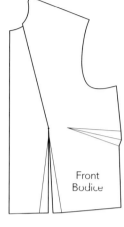

Figure 2

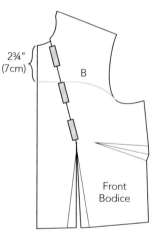

2¾" (7cm)

Figure 3

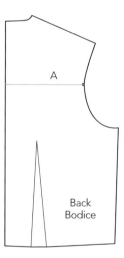

Figure 4

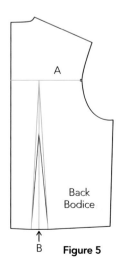

Figure 5

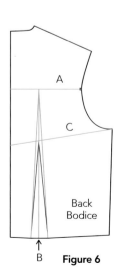

Figure 6

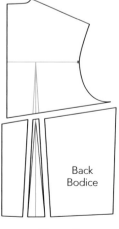

Figure 7

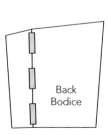

Figure 8

c. Redraw the waist dart lines from the bottom of the dart legs to touch the point where line B touches line A (**Figure 5**).

d. Draw a line (C) from the bottom point of the armhole to the center back that touches the original top of the waist dart (**Figure 6**).

e. Cut the bodice pattern on line C and the new waist dart legs below line C (**Figure 7**).

f. Remove the dart piece and tape the remaining back bodice pieces together (**Figure 8**).

4. Cut one front bodice piece and one back bodice piece on the fold out of outer fabric. The back bodice edge, not the center line, should be placed on the fold of the fabric. Cut one front bodice piece and one back bodice piece on the fold out of lining fabric. Mark the point where the back bodice pieces are taped together on the top edge; this is where the straps will attach.

5. Cut two straps 2" (5.1cm) wide by 18" (45.7cm) long.

6. Cut two skirt panels that are each 0.75 times the waist measurement in width plus 1" (2.6cm), and maxi length (see the skirt measurement guide in Chapter 1).

7. Measure the top edge of the back bodice and cut a piece of elastic to this length multiplied by 0.8 (**Figure 9**).

8. Turn the back bodice right-side out and press.

9. Sew the darts on the front bodice and lining (**Figure 10**).

10. Sew the bodice back to the bodice front along the right side seam, right sides together (**Figure 11**). Repeat with the lining. Baste the left bodice seam together; this seam will have the zipper later.

11. Finish the side edges of the skirt with an overlock stitch or faux overlock stitch.

12. Place the two skirt panels right sides together. Measure down from the top and mark each side at the knee length measurement (see the skirt measurement guide in Chapter 1).

13. Stitch the skirt panels together on the right edge. Press this seam open.

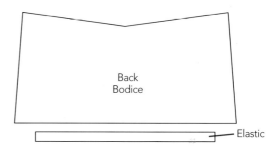

Figure 9

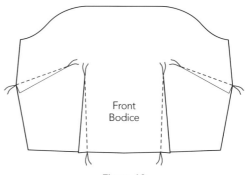

Figure 10

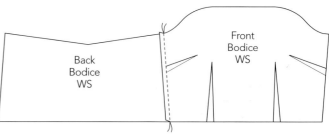

Figure 11

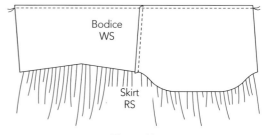

Figure 12

14. Gather the top edge of the skirt to match the width of the bodice at the waistline.

15. Sew the bodice to the skirt along the waistline, right sides together (**Figure 12**). Press the waistline seam toward the bodice.

16. Fold the dress right sides together and insert the zipper in the left side seam (**Figure 13**). Make sure to sew the seam only to the knee-length mark.

17. Press the skirt side seams open again. On the wrong side of the skirt, starting at the bottom, fold the seam allowances under, so that the raw edges meet the sewn seam. Pin. Stitch these edges to secure around the slits in the skirt (**Figure 14**).

18. Press the straps in half, wrong sides together, matching long edges. Open the straps. Press raw edges toward the crease line, wrong sides together. Then press again on the original crease line. Your straps should now be ½" (1.3cm) wide. Topstitch down each side of the strap to finish.

19. Pin the straps to the bodice front, directly above each waist dart point, with the straps pointing down. Baste in place.

20. Press the bottom edge of the lining ⅜" (1cm) to the wrong side.

21. Unzip the dress. Pin the bodice lining to the bodice along the neckline edge, right sides together. The lining should extend beyond the zipper ½" (1.3cm) on each side. Stitch the lining to the bodice, leaving ½" (1.3cm) wide openings at the strap marks on the bodice back (**Figure 15**).

22. Turn the lining to the inside of the dress. Press the neckline.

23. Push the straps into the openings on the back bodice. Pin. Try the dress on and adjust the straps as needed, noting that the back bodice will still be loose in the center. Topstitch the neckline edge of the dress, securing the back straps in the process.

24. Stitch another line across the back bodice ½" (1.3cm) below the topstitching. Insert the elastic through this channel. Stitch the elastic to the right side seam allowance and zipper tape of the dress (**Figure 16**).

25. Turn the raw side edges of the lining ½" (1.3cm) to the wrong side and pin, sandwiching the zipper between the lining and the outer fabric. Stitch over the zipper line again, securing the lining.

26. Pin the bottom folded edge of the lining over the waistline seam (**Figure 17**).

27. On the right side of the dress, stitch in the ditch of the waistline seam to secure the lining, or secure with a slipstitch (**Figure 18**).

28. Turn the bottom edge of the skirt ½" (1.3cm) to the wrong side twice and press to form a hem. Stitch the hem.

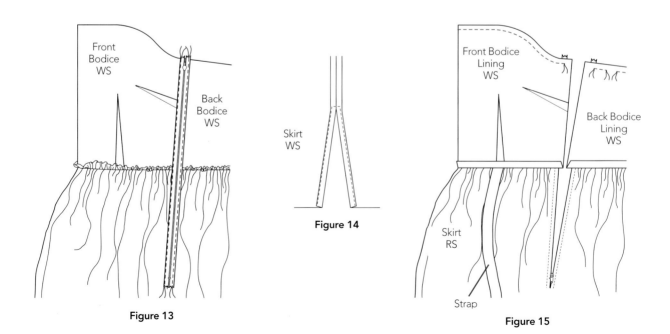

Front Bodice WS

Back Bodice WS

Figure 13

Skirt WS

Figure 14

Front Bodice Lining WS

Back Bodice Lining WS

Skirt RS

Strap

Figure 15

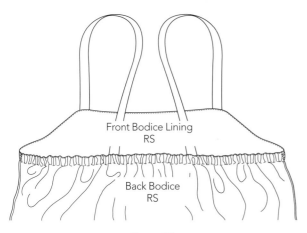

Figure 16

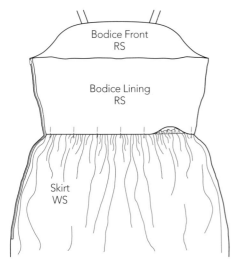

Figure 17

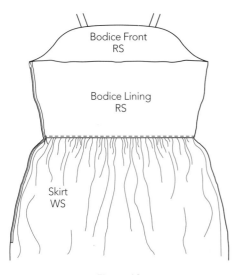

Figure 18

Balcones dress

For your little bohemian, this pretty dress has a tie-shoulder crossover top and tiered skirt. Paired with sandals, it's the perfect outfit for twirling in while strolling down the sidewalk.

Front

Back

Materials

FABRIC
Shown: Quilting weight cotton

Dress Size	44/45" (111.8/114.3cm)	or	58/60" (147.3/152.4cm)
2T	2⅓ yd (2.1m)		1¾ yd (1.6m)
3T	2½ yd (2.3m)		2 yd (1.8m)
4T	2½ yd (2.3m)		2 yd (1.8m)
5	2½ yd (2.3m)		2 yd (1.8m)
6	2½ yd (2.3m)	or	2½ yd (2.3m)
8	3½ yd (3.2m)		3½ yd (3.2m)
10	3½ yd (3.2m)		3½ yd (3.2m)
12	3½ yd (3.2m)		3½ yd (3.2m)

NOTES
½" (1.3cm) seams used unless otherwise noted.

Refer to Chapter 1 for basic sewing techniques and information on customizing fit.

Balcones Dress

1. Trace off the front bodice piece, then flip it over, lining it up to the center front line and trace again, so that you have a full bodice to start with. Repeat this process when tracing the back bodice, making sure to remove the amount added along the center back for the zipper.

2. Modify the front bodice.

   a. Draw a horizontal line at the level of the armscye.

   b. Measure from line A to the bodice bottom. Draw a horizontal line (B) halfway between line A and the waistline (**Figure 1**).

   c. Measure out ½" (1.3cm) from the bodice at line B on each side. Draw a line from the point of the armscye to this mark (C) (**Figure 1**).

   d. Draw a diagonal line (D) from the point of the shoulder to 1" (2.6cm) above mark C at the opposite side (**Figure 1**).

   e. Measure the shoulder and mark the midpoint. Draw a 6" (15.2cm) line (E) straight up from this point (**Figure 2**).

   f. Draw a horizontal line (F) at the top of line E.

   g. On either side of line E draw a line (G) straight up from the midpoint of the armscye and straight up from the shoulder point until line F is reached (**Figure 2**).

   h. Cut out the front bodice pattern following lines B, D, G, F and the diagonal extending from mark C (**Figure 3**).

3. Modify the back bodice, repeating steps 2a–h from the front bodice on the back bodice.

4. Cut four of the front and four of the back bodice pattern pieces out of main fabric (mirrored), giving you two of each side for the front and for the back.

5. For the gathered skirt, take the maxi length (see the skirt measurement chart in Chapter 1) and divide by 9. Call this number A. Cut these three sections that you will ultimately piece together:

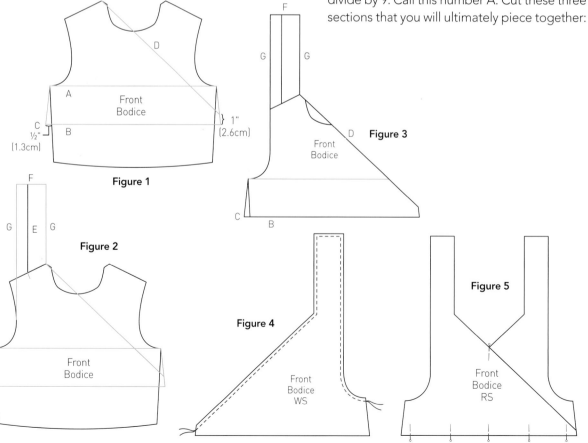

Figure 1

Figure 2

Figure 3

Figure 4

Figure 5

Top tier: 2 × A tall, and 1.5 times the waist width.

Middle tier: 3 × A tall, and 1.5 times the width of the top tier.

Bottom tier: 4 × A tall, and 1.5 times the width of the middle tier.

6. Place two front bodice panels right sides together and stitch the neckline, strap, and armscye edges. Clip corners and curves and turn the piece right-side out; press. Repeat with the other bodice front and bodice back pieces (**Figure 4**).

7. Place one front bodice on top of the other, matching the side edges, and pin together (**Figure 5**). Repeat with the back bodice pieces.

8. On the left side of the bodice match the outer front to the outer back bodice pieces at the side seam edges, sandwiching short edges (from the inner front and back bodice pieces) between them. On the right side of the bodice, match the inner front to the inner back bodice pieces at the side seams, sandwiching short edges (from the outer front and back bodice pieces) between them. This will cause a twisting of the inner fabric because of the overlapped fronts. Sew each side seam (**Figure 6**). Fold the side seams down, so seam allowances are inside the bodice.

9. Sew each skirt tier into a loop by folding right sides together and matching short edges. Sew gathering stitches along the top edge of each tier (**Figure 7**).

10. Gather the top edge of the top tier to match the waistline of the bodice (**Figure 8**).

11. Place the bodice and skirt right sides together, matching waistline edges, and stitch. Finish this seam. (*Note: The dress might be quite bulky at the side seams; you may need to hand crank your machine at this point to sew.*)

12. Gather the top edge of the middle tier to match the bottom edge of the top tier. Place the two tiers right sides together, matching edges, and stitch. Finish this seam (**Figure 9**).

13. Gather the top edge of the bottom tier to match the bottom edge of the middle tier. Place the two tiers right sides together, matching edges, and stitch. Finish this seam (**Figure 10**).

14. Turn the bottom edge of the bottom tier ½" (1.3cm) to the wrong side twice and stitch to form a hem.

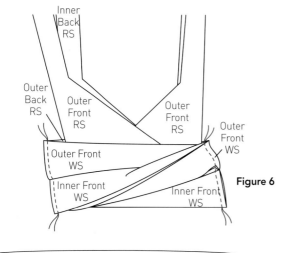

Figure 6

Figure 7

Figure 8

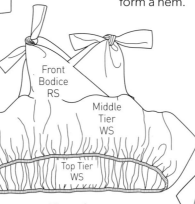
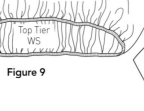

Figure 9

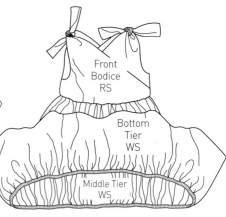

Figure 10

Olive dress

Sweet tie shoulders and a flattering circle skirt make this a classic summer silhouette. Whether on a date or at an event, you're sure to be in style.

Front

Back

Materials

FABRIC
Shown: Cotton eyelet

Dress Size	44/45" (111.8/114.3cm)	or	58/60" (147.3/152.4cm)
0	3¾ yd (3.4m)		2¼ yd (2.1m)
2	3¾ yd (3.4m)		2¼ yd (2.1m)
4	3¾ yd (3.4m)		2¼ yd (2.1m)
6	3¾ yd (3.4m)		2¼ yd (2.1m)
8	3¾ yd (3.4m)		3¾ yd (3.4m)
10	3¾ yd (3.4m)		3¾ yd (3.4m)
12	3¾ yd (3.4m)	or	3¾ yd (3.4m)
14	4⅔ yd (4.3m)		4⅔ yd (4.3m)
16	4⅔ yd (4.3m)		4⅔ yd (4.3m)
18	4⅔ yd (4.3m)		4⅔ yd (4.3m)
20	4⅔ yd (4.3m)		4⅔ yd (4.3m)
22	4⅔ yd (4.3m)		4⅔ yd (4.3m)

NOTIONS
14" (35.6cm) zipper

1 package of double-fold bias tape

NOTES
½" (1.3cm) seams used unless otherwise noted.

Refer to Chapter 1 for basic sewing techniques and information on customizing fit.

Olive Dress

1. Trace off the front and back bodice pieces.

2. Modify the front bodice.

   a. Make a mark on the neckline at about the halfway point of the curve. Draw a line (A) from here to the bust point (**Figure 1**).

   b. Cut through the center of the waist dart, to but not through the bust point (**Figure 2**).

   c. Cut the line from the neckline, to but not through the bust point (**Figure 2**).

   d. Rotate the top half of the bodice so that the neckline overlaps ½" (1.3cm). This will widen the waist dart (**Figure 2**).

   e. Make a mark 1" (2.6cm) in from the shoulder point. Redraw the armscye curve (B) (**Figure 3**).

   f. Make a mark 1½" (3.8cm) down from the neckline. Redraw the neckline (C) to meet the new shoulder point (**Figure 3**).

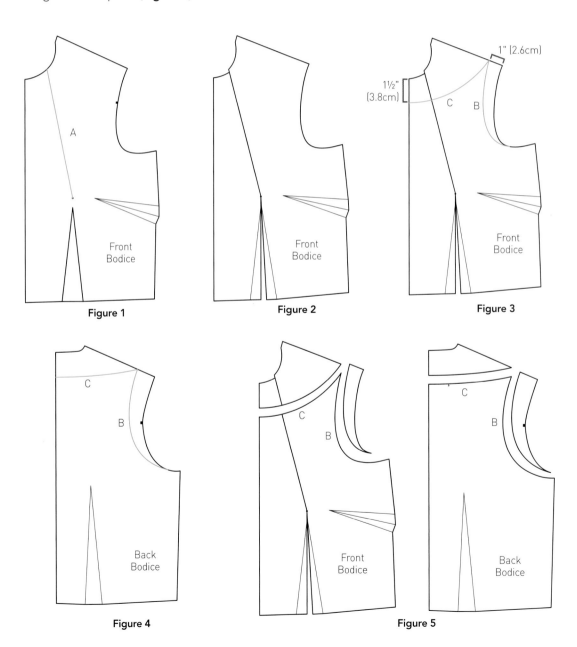

Figure 1

Figure 2

Figure 3

Figure 4

Figure 5

3. Modify the back bodice, repeating steps 2e–f from the front bodice on the back bodice (**Figure 4**).

4. Cut front and back bodice pattern pieces following lines B and C (**Figure 5**); these will be strapless.

5. Cut the front and back bodice pieces on the fold out of main fabric.

6. Measure the new front and back armscye, and add these numbers together. Add 18" (45.7cm) to that number and cut two ½" (1.3cm) wide double-fold bias tape straps this length.

7. Measure the front neckline and double that number. Add 1" (2.6cm) and cut a piece of ½" (1.3cm) wide double-fold bias tape to this length for the front neckline. Repeat this process for the back neckline.

8. For the skirt, cut a circle skirt to knee length (see the skirt measurement guide in Chapter 1). Depending on your fabric, you may need to cut two half-circle skirt panels to get to the correct size and length (see "Circle skirts" in Chapter 1). Open the skirt to a half circle, then cut along one fold so you can open the skirt. If you have cut two half panels, stitch them right sides together along one side seam. Finish this seam.

9. Sew the darts on the front and back bodice pieces.

10. Sew the front bodice to the back bodice at the left side seam (**Figure 6**). Finish this seam.

11. Open the circle skirt. Place the bodice right sides together with the skirt, matching the waist edges. If your skirt has another seam, match this one to the side seam of the bodice. If your skirt ended up too wide for your bodice, trim the skirt along the straight seam lines. If your skirt is not quite wide enough, trim a very small amount (¼" [6mm] to start) off the skirt waistline—this will help the skirt match the bodice. Finish this seam (**Figure 7**).

12. Fold the dress right sides together, matching the waist seam. Pin the side seam. Stitch the top 1" (2.6cm) of the seam from the armscye down, back-stitch, baste the next 13" (33cm), backstitch, then finish stitching the rest of the seam with a normal stitch length.

13. Insert a zipper in the side seam 1" (2.6cm) below the armscye edge (**Figure 8**).

14. With the dress right sides out, unfold the bias tape for the front neckline and pin along the neckline. Stitch in the crease closest to the raw edge (**Figure 9**). The bias tape should be slightly longer than the neckline.

15. Fold the bias tape to the wrong side, making sure to cover the seam from step 14. Stitch on the bias tape edge on the right side, close to the seam, making sure to catch the tape on the wrong side. Trim the edges of the tape to match the neckline of the dress (**Figure 10**).

16. Repeat steps 14–15 with the back bodice (**Figure 11**).

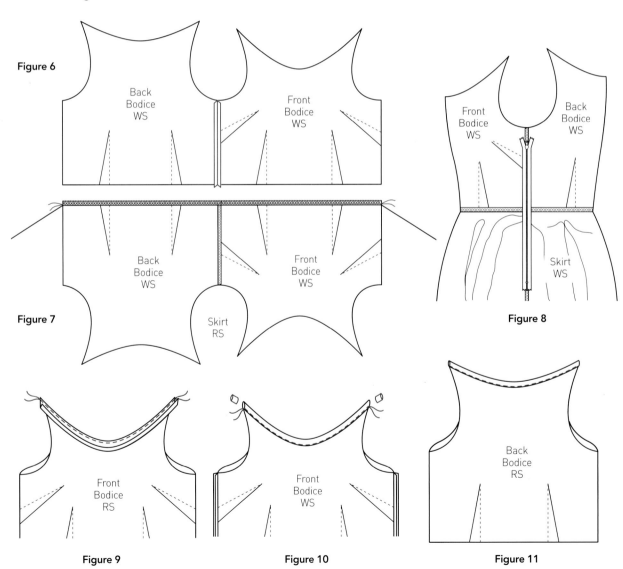

Figure 6

Back Bodice WS

Front Bodice WS

Back Bodice WS

Front Bodice WS

Figure 7

Skirt RS

Front Bodice WS

Back Bodice WS

Skirt WS

Figure 8

Front Bodice RS

Figure 9

Front Bodice WS

Figure 10

Back Bodice RS

Figure 11

17. Fold the bodice to work with one armscye at a time as you add each strap. Take a strap and match the strap center with a side seam. Unfold the bias tape and pin along the armscye. Stitch in the crease closest to the raw edge (**Figure 12**).

18. Fold the bias tape to the wrong side, making sure to cover the side seam. Stitch on the bias tape edge on the right side, close to the seam, making sure to catch the tape on the wrong side (**Figure 13**). Continue to stitch the edges of the bias tape together to form the straps. Trim threads and knot the strap ends to prevent fraying.

19. Hem the skirt.

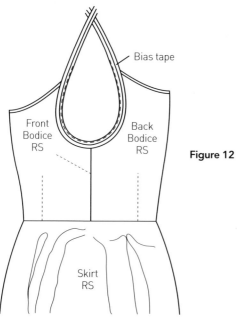

Bias tape

Front Bodice RS

Back Bodice RS

Skirt RS

Figure 12

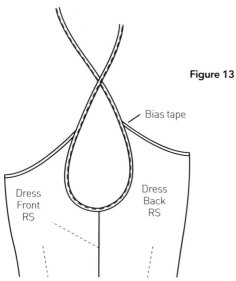

Figure 13

Bias tape

Dress Front RS

Dress Back RS

Palmer dress

Summertime and the living is easy in this tie-shoulder dress. Bias tape makes straps that can coordinate or be sewn in a contrasting color for a fun pop. A ruffled hem keeps it girly and an elastic waist keeps it comfy.

Front

Back

Materials

FABRIC
Shown: Cotton gauze

Dress Size	44/45" (111.8/114.3cm)	or	58/60" (147.3/152.4cm)
2T	2 yd (1.8m)		2 yd (1.8m)
3T	2 yd (1.8m)		2 yd (1.8m)
4T	2 yd (1.8m)		2 yd (1.8m)
5	2 yd (1.8m)		2 yd (1.8m)
6	3¼ yd (3m)	or	2 yd (1.8m)
8	3¼ yd (3m)		2 yd (1.8m)
10	3¼ yd (3m)		2 yd (1.8m)
12	3¼ yd (3m)		2 yd (1.8m)

NOTIONS
1 package of double-fold bias tape

1 yd (0.9m) of ½" (1.3cm) wide elastic

NOTES
½" (1.3cm) seams used unless otherwise noted.

Refer to Chapter 1 for basic sewing techniques and information on customizing fit.

Palmer Dress

1. Trace off the front and back bodice pieces.

2. Modify the front bodice (**Figure 1**).

   a. Redraw the side seam (A) at a 90° angle from the bottom of the armscye (instead of angling in toward the waist).

   b. Draw a horizontal line (B) at the level of the bottom of the armhole.

   c. Measure vertically between the point of the neckline and line B. Draw a horizontal line (C) one-quarter of the distance from the neckline.

   d. Measure the shoulder seam. Mark the midpoint of the shoulder seam. Draw a line at 90° from the midpoint of the shoulder to line C; the point at which this line touches line C is point D.

   e. From point D, draw an angled line (E) merging with the armscye.

   f. Measure vertically between the point of the neckline and line B. Mark a point one-third of the distance from the neckline, then connect this point to point D in a curve (F) to form the new neckline.

3. Modify the back bodice by repeating steps 2a–f from the front bodice on the back bodice (**Figure 2**).

4. Cut front and back bodice pattern pieces following lines F, E and A (**Figures 1 and 2**); these will be strapless.

5. Cut the front and back bodice pieces on the fold out of main fabric.

6. Measure the new front and back armscye, and add these numbers together. Add 18" (45.7cm) to that number and cut two ½" (1.3cm) wide double-fold bias tape straps this length.

7. Measure the front neckline and double that number. Add 1" (2.6cm) and cut a piece of ½" (1.3cm) wide double-fold bias tape to this length for the front neckline. Repeat for the back neckline.

8. For the skirt, cut a rectangle that is 2 times the waist measurement in width, and maxi length (see the skirt measurement guide in Chapter 1).

9. Cut a ruffle 7" (17.8cm) tall and twice the width of the skirt. You may have to cut two pieces to achieve the width needed.

10. With the front bodice right-side up, unfold the bias tape for the neckline and pin along the neckline. Stitch in the crease closest to the raw edge (**Figure 3**). The bias tape should be slightly longer than the neckline.

11. Fold the bias tape to the wrong side, making sure to cover the seam from step 10. Stitch on the bias tape edge on the right side, close to the seam, making sure to catch the tape on the wrong side (**Figure 4**). Trim the edges of the tape to match the neckline of the dress (**Figure 5**).

12. Repeat steps 10–11 with the back bodice.

13. Place the two bodice pieces right sides together, and sew and finish the side seams (**Figure 6**).

14. Turn the bodice right-side out, then fold the bodice to work with one armscye at a time as you add each strap. Take a strap and match the strap center with a side seam. Unfold the bias tape and pin along the armscye. Stitch in the crease closest to the raw edge (**Figure 7**).

15. Fold the bias tape to the wrong side, making sure to cover the side seam. Stitch on the bias tape edge on the right side, close to the seam, making sure to catch the tape on the wrong side. Continue to stitch the edges of the bias tape together to form the straps (**Figure 8**). Trim threads and knot the strap ends to prevent fraying.

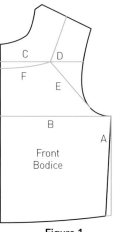

Figure 1

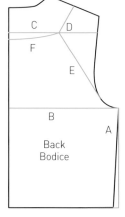

Figure 2

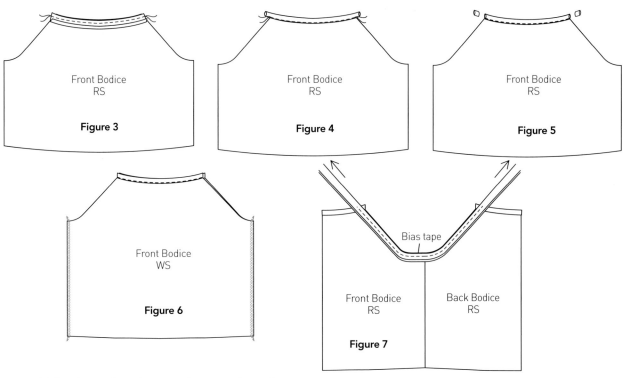

Front Bodice
RS

Figure 3

Front Bodice
RS

Figure 4

Front Bodice
RS

Figure 5

Front Bodice
WS

Figure 6

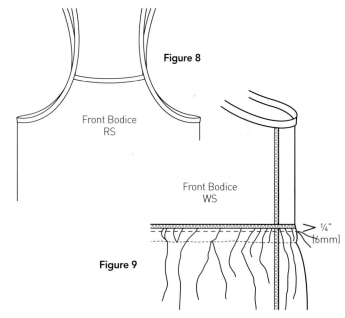

Bias tape

Front Bodice
RS

Back Bodice
RS

Figure 7

Figure 8

Front Bodice
RS

Front Bodice
WS

Figure 9

¼"
(6mm)

16. Fold the skirt right sides together, matching the short edges. Stitch the short edges; finish this seam. Turn one raw edge ¼" (6mm) to the wrong side twice, forming a narrow hem. Stitch the hem.

17. Fold the ruffle right sides together, matching the short edges. Stitch the short edges; finish this seam.

18. Finish both raw edges of the ruffle by turning ¼" (6mm) to the wrong side twice then stitching to form a narrow hem.

19. Gather the ruffle with stitches ½" (1.3cm) from one hemmed edge to the same width as the skirt. Place the ruffle wrong side against the skirt right side and stitch in place over the gathering stitches. The ruffle should hang about ½" (1.3cm) lower than the bottom of the skirt.

20. The skirt seam is the center back. Fold the skirt to mark the center front. Gather the top edge of the skirt to match the width of the bodice at the waistline.

21. Turn the bodice wrong-side out.

22. Put the bodice inside the skirt right sides together, matching waistlines, center back and center front. Stitch this seam using a 1" (2.6cm) seam allowance. Finish this seam with an overlock stitch or faux overlock stitch.

23. Turn the waist seam up toward the bodice. Stitch ¼" (6mm) from the finished seam edge to form a waist casing (**Figure 9**). (*Note:* Make sure to check the bobbin thread color, as this stitching will show on the right side, and make sure that the bodice fabric is smooth and flat when stitching.) Leave an opening to insert elastic.

24. Use a safety pin to insert elastic through the waist casing, then sew the opening closed.

3

City Chic

Sundressing isn't just for the weekends. Carry this effortless style into the work week as well with the dresses in this section.

Metropolitan dress

Uptown or downtown, this dress is a no-fuss staple for summer days spent playing hopscotch, jumping rope and gallivanting around the city. Button shoulders add a cosmopolitan detail and the A-line shape keeps it city chic.

Front

Back

Materials

FABRIC
Shown: Quilting weight cotton

Dress Size	44/45" (111.8/114.3cm)	or	58/60" (147.3/152.4cm)
2T	1½ yd (1.4m)		1½ yd (1.4m)
3T	1⅔ yd (1.5m)		1⅔ yd (1.5m)
4T	1⅔ yd (1.5m)		1⅔ yd (1.5m)
5	1⅔ yd (1.5m)		1⅔ yd (1.5m)
6	1¾ yd (1.6m)	or	1¾ yd (1.6m)
8	1¾ yd (1.6m)		1¾ yd (1.6m)
10	1¾ yd (1.6m)		1¾ yd (1.6m)
12	1¾ yd (1.6m)		1¾ yd (1.6m)

NOTIONS
Two ½" (1.3cm) buttons

NOTES
Fabric amounts listed include enough for lining in the same fabric. Recalculate if using different material for lining.

½" (1.3cm) seams used unless otherwise noted.

Refer to Chapter 1 for basic sewing techniques and information on customizing fit.

Metropolitan Dress

1. Trace off the front and back bodice pieces.

2. Modify the front bodice (**Figure 1**).

   a. Redraw the side seam at a 90° angle (A) from the bottom of the armscye (instead of angling in toward the waist).

   b. Draw a horizontal line (B) at the level of the bottom of the armhole.

   c. Measure vertically between the neckline and line B. Mark a point a quarter of the way down from the neckline. Draw a horizontal line (C) at this point for the new neckline.

   d. Measure the shoulder seam. Mark the mid-point of the shoulder seam. Measure 1¼" (3.2cm) to either side of this mark for the straps. Connect diagonal strap lines (D) to the neck-line. The straps should remain 2½" (6.4cm) wide—1¼" (3.2cm) to each side of the center.

   e. Find the outer point where the strap meets the new neckline (C). Draw a diagonal line (E) from this point sloping down toward the armhole.

3. Modify the back bodice by repeating steps 2a–e from the front bodice on the back bodice (**Figure 2**).

4. Cut the front and back bodice pattern pieces. Cut the strap piece off the front bodice (**Figure 3**). Tape the front strap piece to the back bodice and add a ½" (1.3cm) seam allowance to the top of the strap (**Figure 4**).

5. Cut the front and back bodice pieces on the fold out of main fabric and lining.

6. Cut the skirt to 1.5 times the waist measurement in width, and knee length (see the skirt measurement guide in Chapter 1).

7. Pin the back bodice lining to the bodice back, right sides together, and stitch the neckline and armhole edges (**Figure 5**). Clip corners.

8. Pin the front bodice lining to the bodice front, right sides together, and stitch the neckline and armhole edges (**Figure 6**). Clip corners. Turn right-side out and press.

9. Place the bodice back flat and fold the outer sides up (**Figure 7**). Open the front bodice and place it right sides together with the back bodice. Match the side seam edges and armhole seams of the outer and lining fabrics to each other. Stitch lining and outer fabric in one seam for each side (**Figure 8**). Turn the bodice right-side out and press (**Figure 9**).

10. Stitch two horizontal buttonholes on the bodice front, parallel to the neck edge and about ¼" (6mm) in from the outer neck edges.

11. Fold the skirt right sides together, matching the short edges. Stitch the short edges; finish this seam. Turn one raw edge ½" (1.3cm) to the wrong side twice, forming a hem. Stitch the hem.

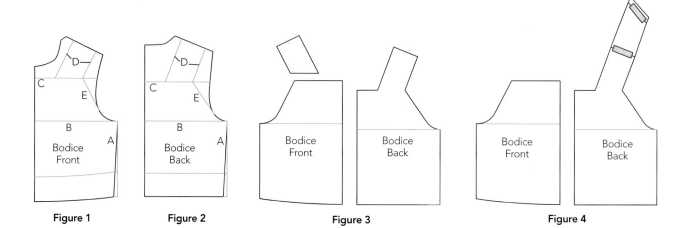

Figure 1   Figure 2   Figure 3   Figure 4

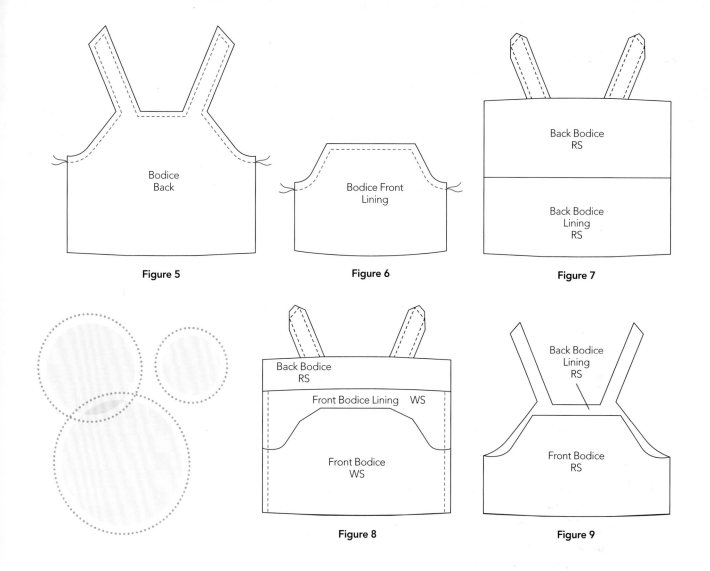

Figure 5

Bodice
Back

Figure 6

Bodice Front
Lining

Figure 7

Back Bodice
RS

Back Bodice
Lining
RS

Figure 8

Back Bodice
RS

Front Bodice Lining   WS

Front Bodice
WS

Figure 9

Back Bodice
Lining
RS

Front Bodice
RS

12. Turn the skirt right-side out. Gather the top edges to match the width of the bodice at the waistline.

13. Turn the bodice lining side out. Press the bottom edge of the lining ⅜" (1cm) in to the wrong side.

14. Put the skirt inside the bodice, matching waistlines, center back and center front. Pin bodice outer fabric to the skirt and stitch (**Figure 10**).

15. Pin the folded edge of the lining over the waistline seam. On the right side of the dress, stitch in the ditch of the waistline seam to secure the lining or use a slipstitch.

16. Stitch buttons onto the back straps.

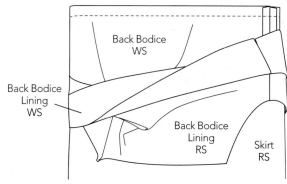

Back Bodice
WS

Back Bodice
Lining
WS

Back Bodice
Lining
RS

Skirt
RS

Figure 10

SoCo dress

As hip and happening as the Austin area it's named for, this dress can be at home anywhere from an art gallery to the park, depending on fabric choices. The tulip-shaped skirt keeps it edgy while the traditional bodice keeps it classy.

Front

Back

Materials

FABRIC

Shown: Polyester georgette over a polyester charmeuse half slip*

Dress Size	44/45" (111.8/114.3cm)	or	58/60" (147.3/152.4cm)
0	3¼ yd (3m)		3¼ yd (3m)
2	3¼ yd (3m)		3¼ yd (3m)
4	3¼ yd (3m)		3¼ yd (3m)
6	3¼ yd (3m)		3¼ yd (3m)
8	3¼ yd (3m)		3¼ yd (3m)
10	3¼ yd (3m)		3¼ yd (3m)
12	3¼ yd (3m)	or	3¼ yd (3m)
14	4 yd (3.7m)		3¼ yd (3m)
16	4 yd (3.7m)		3¼ yd (3m)
18	4 yd (3.7m)		3¼ yd (3m)
20	4 yd (3.7m)		3¼ yd (3m)
22	4 yd (3.7m)		3¼ yd (3m)

NOTIONS
14" (35.6cm) zipper

NOTES
½" (1.3cm) seams used unless otherwise noted.

Refer to Chapter 1 for basic sewing techniques and information on customizing fit.

*Dress shown is made with sheer fabric and has a coordinating half slip requiring an additional 1¼ yd (1.1m) of fabric. To make, cut the slip fabric to knee length and 1.5 times the waist measurement, then gather and attach to a ½" (1.3cm) wide elastic strip that is 1" (2.6cm) less than the waist measurement.

SoCo Dress

1. Trace off the front and back bodice pieces.

2. Modify the front bodice.

   a. Make a mark on the neckline at about the halfway point of the curve. Draw a line (A) from here to the bust point (**Figure 1**).

   b. Cut through the center of the waist dart, to but not through the bust point (**Figure 2**).

   c. Cut the line from the neckline, to but not through the bust point (**Figure 2**).

   d. Rotate the top half of the bodice so that the neckline overlaps ½" (1.3cm). This will widen the waist dart (**Figure 2**).

   e. Make a mark on the center front 2¾" (7cm) down from the neckline edge. Draw a curved line (B) from this mark to the armhole for the new neckline (**Figure 3**).

   f. Cut the bodice along line B.

3. Modify the back bodice.

   a. Draw a 90° line (A) from the mark on the armhole of the back bodice to the center back (**Figure 4**).

   b. Extend the center line (B) of the waist dart straight up to touch line A (**Figure 5**).

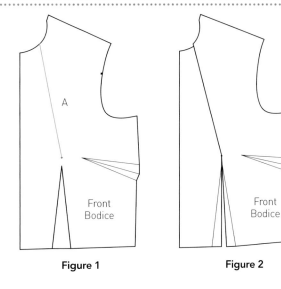

Figure 1

Figure 2

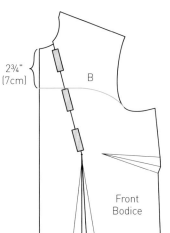

2¾"
(7cm)

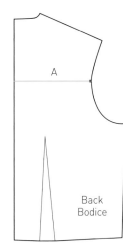

Figure 3

Figure 4

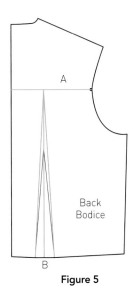

Figure 5

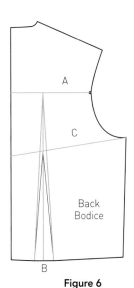

Figure 6

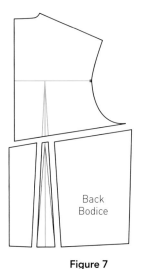

Figure 7

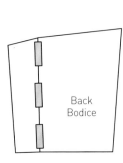

Figure 8

c. Redraw the waist dart lines from the bottom of the dart legs to touch the point where line B touches line A (**Figure 5**).

d. Draw a line (C) from the bottom point of the armhole to the center back that touches the original top of the waist dart (**Figure 6**).

e. Cut the bodice pattern on line C and the new waist dart legs below line C (**Figure 7**).

f. Remove the dart piece and tape the remaining back bodice pieces together (**Figure 8**).

4. Cut one front bodice piece on the fold and cut two back bodice pieces (mirrored) out of outer fabric. Cut one front bodice piece on the fold and cut two back bodice pieces (mirrored) out of lining fabric. Mark the point where the back bodice pieces are taped together on the top edge; this is where the straps will attach.

5. Cut two straps 2" (5.1cm) wide by 18" (45.7cm) long.

6. Cut three rectangular skirt panels to 1.5 times the waist measurement in width, and knee length (see the skirt measurement guide in Chapter 1).

7. Sew the darts on the front bodice and lining (**Figure 9**).

8. Sew the two bodice back pieces at the center back seam. Sew the bodice back to the bod-

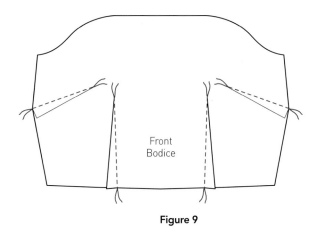

Figure 9

ice front along the right side seam, right sides together (**Figure 10**). Repeat with lining. Baste the left bodice seam together; this seam will have the zipper later.

9. Lay two of the skirt panels on top of each other and cut off one corner in a curve (**Figure 11**).

10. Finish the straight short edges of these two panels and the short raw edges of the remaining skirt panel with an overlock stitch or faux overlock stitch.

11. Sew each of these panels right sides together with the remaining panel in the center, making sure to use a basting stitch for the top 5" (12.7cm) on what will be the left side seam of the skirt (**Figure 12**).

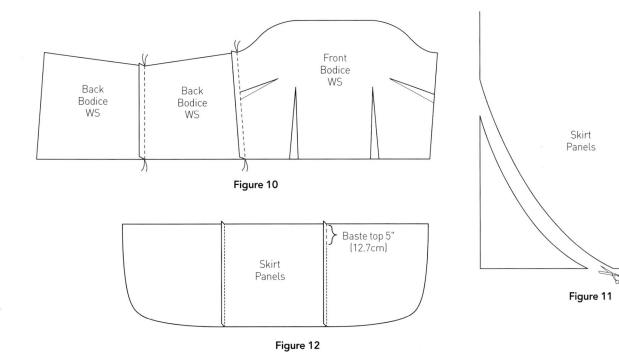

Figure 10

Figure 11

Figure 12

12. Turn the bottom edge of the skirt ¼" (6mm) to the wrong side twice to form a narrow hem. Stitch.

13. Overlap the skirt front so that the right panel is over the left panel (**Figure 13**).

14. Gather the top edge of the skirt to match the width of the bodice at the waistline.

15. Sew the bodice to the skirt along the waistline, right sides together (**Figure 14**). Press the waistline seam toward the bodice.

16. Insert the zipper in the left side seam.

17. Press the straps in half, wrong sides together, matching long edges. Open straps. Press raw edges toward the crease line, wrong sides together. Then press again on the original crease line. Your straps should now be ½" (1.3cm) wide. Topstitch down each side of the strap to finish.

18. Pin the straps to the bodice front, directly above each waist dart point, with the straps pointing down. Baste in place.

19. Press the bottom edge of the lining ⅜" (1cm) to the wrong side.

20. Pin the bodice lining to the bodice along the neckline edge, right sides together. The lining should extend beyond the zipper ½" (1.3cm) on each side (**Figure 15**). Stitch the lining to the bodice along the neckline, leaving ½" (1.3cm) wide openings at the strap marks on the bodice back.

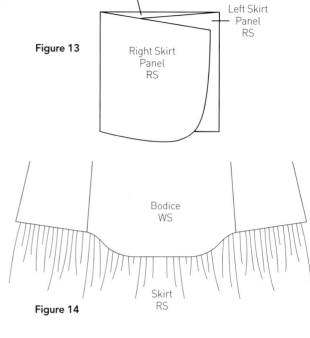

Figure 13

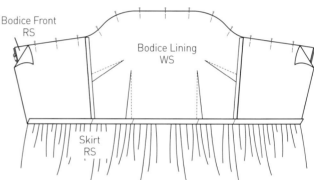

Figure 14

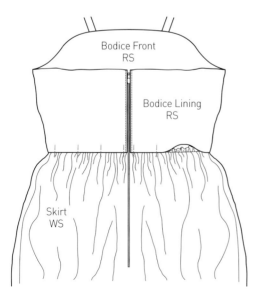

Figure 16

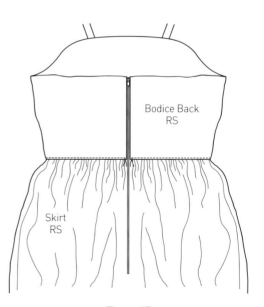

Figure 17

Figure 15

21. Turn the lining to the inside of the dress. Press the neckline.

22. Turn the center back edges of the lining ½" (1.3cm) to the wrong side and pin, sandwiching the zipper between the lining and the outer fabric. Stitch over the zipper line again, securing the lining.

23. Pin the folded edge of the lining over the waistline seam (Figure 16).

24. On the right side of the dress, stitch in the ditch of the waistline seam to secure the lining, or secure with a slipstitch (Figure 17).

25. Push the straps into the openings on the back bodice. Pin. Try the dress on and adjust the straps as needed. Topstitch the neckline edge of the dress, securing the back straps in the process.

Parlin dress

With a contrasting faux collar and sash, the Parlin Dress can be a work-appropriate staple for warm weather. Have fun playing with color combinations on this retro dress.

Front

Back

Materials

FABRIC
Shown: Cotton pique (main) and cotton broadcloth (contrast)

Dress Size	Main Fabric 44/45" (111.8/ 114.3cm)		Main Fabric 58/60" (147.3/ 152.4cm)	Contrast Fabric (either width)
0	3 yd (2.7m)	or	2 yd (1.8m)	½ yd (0.5m)
2	3 yd (2.7m)		2 yd (1.8m)	½ yd (0.5m)
4	3 yd (2.7m)		2 yd (1.8m)	½ yd (0.5m)
6	3 yd (2.7m)		2 yd (1.8m)	½ yd (0.5m)
8	3 yd (2.7m)		3 yd (2.7m)	½ yd (0.5m)
10	3 yd (2.7m)		3 yd (2.7m)	½ yd (0.5m)
12	3 yd (2.7m)	or	3 yd (2.7m)	½ yd (0.5m)
14	4 yd (3.7m)		3 yd (2.7m)	½ yd (0.5m)
16	4 yd (3.7m)		3 yd (2.7m)	½ yd (0.5m)
18	4 yd (3.7m)		3 yd (2.7m)	¾ yd (0.7m)
20	4 yd (3.7m)		3 yd (2.7m)	¾ yd (0.7m)
22	4 yd (3.7m)		3 yd (2.7m)	¾ yd (0.7m)

NOTIONS
22" (55.9cm) zipper

NOTES
Main fabric amounts listed include enough for lining in the same fabric. Recalculate if using different material for lining.

½" (1.3cm) seams used unless otherwise noted.

Refer to Chapter 1 for basic sewing techniques and information on customizing fit.

Parlin Dress

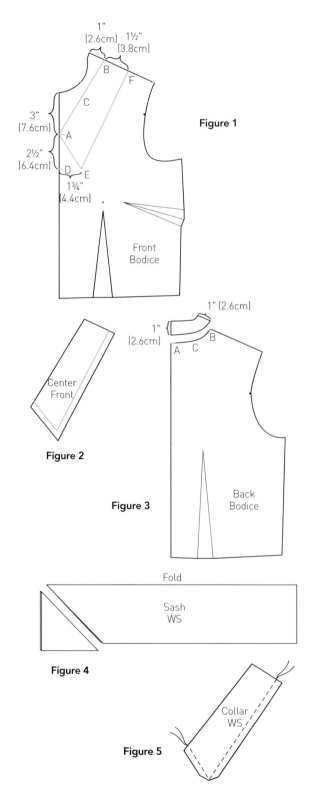

Figure 1

Figure 2

Figure 3

Figure 4

Figure 5

1. Trace off the front and back bodice pieces.

2. Modify the front bodice (**Figure 1**).

    a. Make a mark (A) 3" (7.6cm) down from the neckline.

    b. Make a mark (B) 1" (2.6cm) in from the neckline edge on the shoulder.

    c. Draw a line (C) between marks A and B.

    d. Measure down 2½" (6.4cm) from mark A and make a mark (D) on the center front.

    e. Measure in 1¾" (4.4cm) horizontally from mark D and make another mark (E).

    f. Connect marks A and E.

    g. Measure 1½" (3.8cm) down the shoulder seam from mark B and make a mark (F).

    h. Connect marks E and F. This completes the outline of the collar.

    i. Cut the bodice along line C.

    j. Trace off the collar and add seam allowances to the outer two edges as shown (**Figure 2**).

3. Modify the back bodice (**Figure 3**).

    a. Make a mark (A) 1" (2.6cm) down from the neckline.

    b. Make a mark (B) 1" (2.6cm) in from the neckline on the shoulder.

    c. Draw a curved line (C) between marks A and B.

    d. Cut the bodice along line C.

4. Cut the front bodice piece and two back bodice pieces (mirrored) on the fold out of main fabric and lining.

5. Cut a front skirt panel that is the waist measurement in width plus 1" (2.6cm) and two back skirt panels that are one-half the waist measurement in width plus 1" (2.6cm). Make all panels knee length (see the skirt measurement guide in Chapter 1).

6. Cut a sash 9" (22.9cm) wide and 3 times the waist length out of contrast fabric. You will probably need to piece fabric to reach this length.

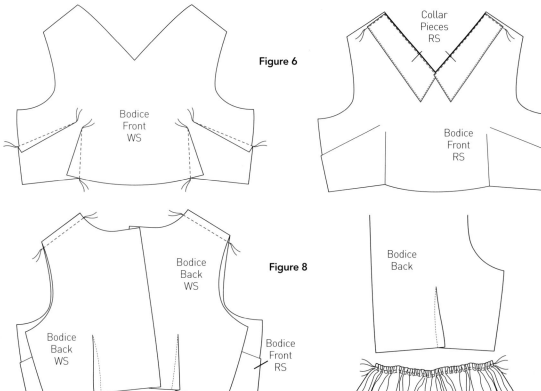

Figure 6

Bodice
Front
WS

Collar
Pieces
RS

Figure 7

Bodice
Front
RS

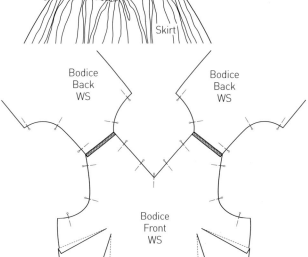

Figure 8

Bodice
Back
WS

Bodice
Back
WS

Bodice
Front
RS

Bodice
Back

Figure 9

Skirt

Bodice
Back
WS

Bodice
Back
WS

Bodice
Front
WS

Figure 10

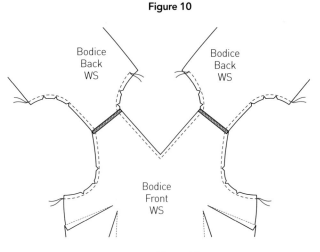

Bodice
Back
WS

Bodice
Back
WS

Bodice
Front
WS

Figure 11

7. Cut four collar pieces (mirrored, two on each side) out of contrast fabric.

8. Finish all skirt panel side edges with an overlock stitch or faux overlock stitch.

9. Fold the sash right sides together, matching long edges. Cut each short edge at a 45° angle (**Figure 4**). Stitch the sash along the raw edges, leaving an opening midway down the long side to turn the sash. Turn the sash right side out and press. Topstitch the sash edges, closing the opening in the process.

10. Place two collar pieces right sides together and stitch the two outer edges. Clip corners and turn the collar right-side out. Press and topstitch the outer edges (**Figure 5**). Repeat with the other two collar pieces.

11. Stitch the darts in the bodice front and backs (**Figure 6**). Repeat with the front lining.

12. Press the bottom edges of the lining pieces ⅜" (1cm) to the wrong side.

13. Lay collar pieces along the neckline edge of the bodice front. They should be ¼" (6mm) away from the shoulder seams so that they overlap at the center front ½" (1.3cm) down from the point of the V (**Figure 7**). Baste the collar in place.

14. Stitch the front and back bodice pieces together at the shoulders (**Figure 8**). Repeat with lining.

15. Sew gathering stitches on the back skirt panels. Gather to match the back bodice (**Figure 9**).

16. Stitch each back skirt panel to a back bodice piece, right sides together. Press seams toward bodice.

17. Place bodice and lining right sides together, matching neckline and armscye edges, and pin (**Figure 10**). Stitch neckline and armhole edges, starting and stopping the neckline stitching ½" (1.3cm) from the center back edge, and clip curves (**Figure 11**). Turn dress right-side out. Press seams.

18. Fold the dress in half, right sides together, matching the center back seam. Fold the lining out of the way. Lay the zipper along the center back seam and make a mark on the skirt just above the zipper stop. Baste from the neckline down to the zipper mark, then stop, backstitch, and change to a regular stitch length for the rest of the seam (**Figure 12**).

19. Insert a zipper in the center back seam (**Figure 13**).

20. Gather the front skirt panel to the same width as the front bodice. Stitch front bodice to skirt at the waistline, right sides together. Press seam toward bodice.

21. Fold the dress to match the side seams, right sides together. Pin the side seams and the lining side seams, matching the waist and armscye seams. Stitch the side seams (**Figure 14**).

22. Fold the lining to the inside of the dress. Press the center back edges of the lining ⅝" (1.6cm) to the wrong side and pin to the back of the zipper. Stitch on the zipper seam line to secure the lining center back.

23. Pin the bottom folded edges of the lining to cover the waistline seam, matching seams and darts. On the front of the dress, stitch in the ditch of the waistline seam to secure the lining, or secure with a slipstitch.

24. Hem the skirt by turning the bottom edge ½" (1.3cm) to the wrong side twice and stitching.

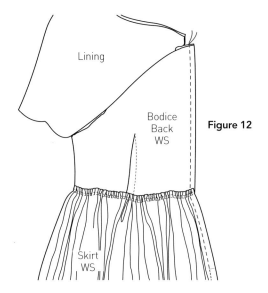

Figure 12

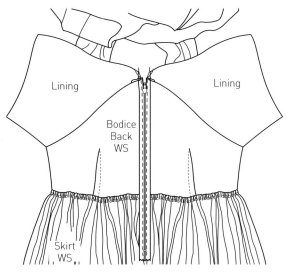

Figure 13

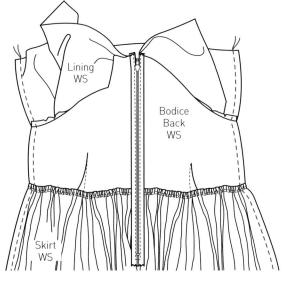

Figure 14

Littlefield dress

Named after a fountain on a university campus near where I live, this smart and stylish dress transitions easily from summertime to schooltime. With a partially pleated skirt and a cute faux button tab detail on the neckline, this dress in a crisp twill is summer preppy at its best.

Front

Back

Materials

FABRIC
Shown: Cotton twill

Dress Size	44/45" (111.8/114.3cm)	or	58/60" (147.3/152.4cm)
2T	2¼ yd (2.1m)		2¼ yd (2.1m)
3T	2¼ yd (2.1m)		2¼ yd (2.1m)
4T	2¼ yd (2.1m)		2¼ yd (2.1m)
5	2¼ yd (2.1m)		2¼ yd (2.1m)
6	2¼ yd (2.1m)	or	2¼ yd (2.1m)
8	2¼ yd (2.1m)		2¼ yd (2.1m)
10	2¼ yd (2.1m)		2¼ yd (2.1m)
12	2¼ yd (2.1m)		2¼ yd (2.1m)

NOTIONS
16" (40.6cm) zipper

Five ⅝"–¾" (1.6cm–1.9cm) buttons

NOTES
Fabric amounts listed include enough for lining in the same fabric. Recalculate if using different material for lining.

½" (1.3cm) seams used unless otherwise noted.

Refer to Chapter 1 for basic sewing techniques and information on customizing fit.

Littlefield Dress

1. Trace off the front and back bodice pieces.

2. Modify the front bodice.

   a. Draw a curved line (A) 1" (2.6cm) away from the neckline, following the curve of the neckline. Cut the bodice along this line (**Figure 1**).

   b. Repeat step 2a on the new neckline (forming line B), but do not cut (**Figure 1**).

   c. Approximately one-third of the way along the newly drawn area, draw in a curved line (C)—this is where the button tab will end (**Figure 1**).

   d. Retrace the entire button tab area onto a new sheet of paper. Then flip the paper, line up the center front line and continue tracing just to the curved area of the button tab. This is the long button tab (**Figure 2**).

   e. Trace an area of the button tab on the bodice from the shoulder to approximately 1" (2.6cm) past line C. This is the short button tab.

   f. Add seam allowances of ½" (1.3cm) all around the button tab pattern pieces, except for the straight short ends (**Figure 3**).

3. Modify the back bodice.

   a. Draw a curved line 1" (2.6cm) away from the neckline, following the curve of the neckline. Cut the bodice along this line (**Figure 4**).

   b. Create the side tab pieces. Make a rectangle 9" (22.9cm) wide and 3½" (8.9cm) tall. Fold the piece in quarters and cut a curve through the four corners to create the curve of the side tabs (**Figure 5**).

4. Cut the front bodice piece on the fold out of main fabric and lining. Cut two back bodice pieces (mirrored) out of main fabric and lining.

5. Cut two long button tabs and two short button tabs (mirrored) out of main fabric.

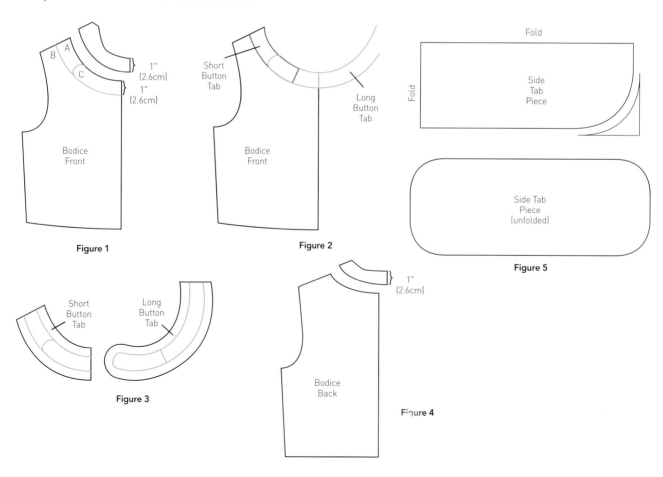

Figure 1

Figure 2

Figure 3

Figure 4

Figure 5

6. Cut four side tabs out of main fabric.

7. Cut a skirt panel that is the waist measurement in width plus 25" (63.5cm), and knee length (see the skirt measurement guide in Chapter 1). If you need to piece fabric to get to this width, cut two back panels that are one-eighth of the waist plus 1" (2.6cm), then cut the remaining three-quarters of the waist amount plus 25" (63.5cm) as one panel.

8. Prepare the skirt. First, if you had to piece the skirt, sew the panels together and finish these seams. Lay the skirt flat, right-side up. Next, finish the center back seam edges with an overlock stitch or faux overlock stitch. Then measure in one-eighth of the waist measurement plus ½" (1.3cm) from the edge and mark the fabric at the top and bottom, then draw a line on the fabric with a water-soluble fabric marker. (*Note:* If you pieced your skirt, this line will land on the seam line. Be sure to test your marker for washability, as you will be marking the front side of the fabric for the pleats.)

9. Next, measure in 1" (2.6cm) from this line and draw another line. Repeat until you have made 18 total lines (including the first line) 1" (2.6cm) apart. Repeat this process working from the other edge of the skirt (**Figure 6**).

10. Fold the skirt wrong sides together on the line closest to the back edge. Press this fold. Move the fold over to match the third line, and press. This creates one pleat with folds on the first two lines. Pin this pleat at the top and bottom of the skirt. Move over to the fourth line and fold the skirt wrong sides together on the line. Press this fold. Move the fold over to match the sixth line, and press. Repeat until you have six pleats on each side of the skirt (**Figure 7**).

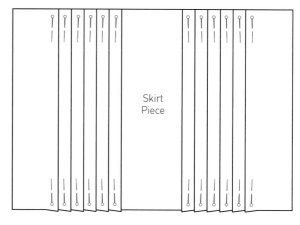

Figure 7

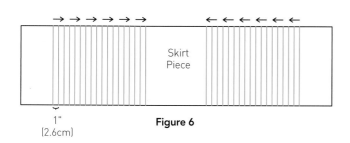

1"
(2.6cm)

Figure 6

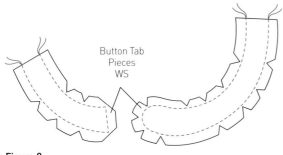

Button Tab
Pieces
WS

Figure 8

Button Tab
Pieces
RS

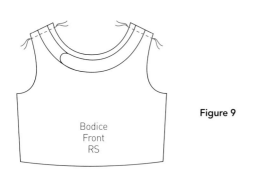

Bodice
Front
RS

Figure 9

Figure 10

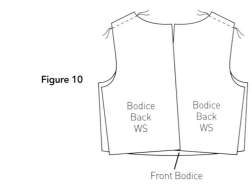

Bodice
Back
WS

Bodice
Back
WS

Front Bodice

Figure 11

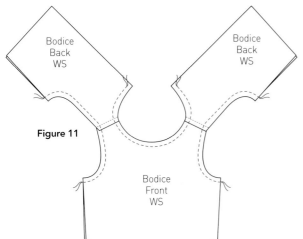

Bodice
Back
WS

Bodice
Back
WS

Bodice
Front
WS

11. Place the long button tab pieces right sides together and sew around the curved edges, then clip corners. Turn and press. Repeat this process with the short button tab pieces, sewing the edge closest to center front closed and leaving the shoulder edge open (**Figure 8**).

12. Place the button tabs on the neckline of the bodice front. Make sure the edges of the tabs are at least ½" (1.3cm) away from both the neckline and the armhole edges. Baste in place at the shoulders (**Figure 9**).

13. Place the front and back bodice pieces right sides together and stitch across the shoulders. Repeat with lining (**Figure 10**).

14. Open the bodice and place the bodice lining right sides together with the bodice, matching all edges. Beginning ½" (1.3cm) in from the center back, stitch around the neckline and armholes, being careful not to catch the button tabs in the seams (**Figure 11**).

15. Clip curves, turn the bodice right-side out and press (**Figure 12**).

16. Fold the bodice right sides together, matching the front and back side seams of the outer fabric to each other and the side seams of the lining together. Match the armscye seams. Stitch the lining and outer fabric in one seam for each side (**Figure 13**). The center back edges of the bodice remain open.

17. Arrange the long button tab over the short button tab on the bodice front. Stitch one button on through the tab layers and outer fabric.

18. Press the bottom edge of the lining ⅜" (1cm) to the wrong side.

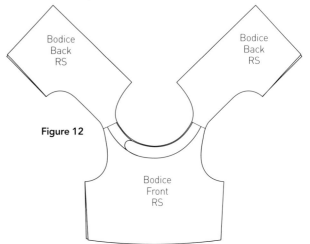

Bodice
Back
RS

Bodice
Back
RS

Figure 12

Bodice
Front
RS

19. Place the outer bodice and skirt right sides together, matching the waistline. Stitch the waistline (**Figure 14**).

20. Fold the dress in half, right sides together, matching the center back seam. Fold the lining out of the way. Lay the zipper along the center back seam and make a mark on the skirt just above the zipper stop. Baste from the neckline down to the zipper mark, then stop, backstitch, and change to a regular stitch length for the rest of the seam (**Figure 15**).

21. Insert the zipper in the center back seam.

22. Fold the lining to the inside of the dress. Press the center back edges of the lining ⅝" (1.6cm) to the wrong side and pin to the back of the zipper. Stitch on the zipper seam line to secure the lining center back.

23. Pin the bottom folded edges of the lining to cover the waistline seam, matching seams and darts. On the front of the dress, stitch in the ditch of the waistline seam to secure the lining, or secure with a slipstitch.

24. Hem the skirt by turning the bottom edge ½" (1.3cm) to the wrong side twice and stitching.

25. Place two side tab pieces right sides together. Stitch around the edges, leaving an opening on the straight edge to turn. Clip corners, turn right-side out and press the tab. Topstitch around the edge of the tab, closing the opening (**Figure 16**).

26. Stitch four buttons onto the skirt at the divisions between the pleated and flat parts of the skirt. Place side tabs around the sides of the dress to mark buttonholes. Stitch four buttonholes and button the side tabs onto the dress (**Figure 17**).

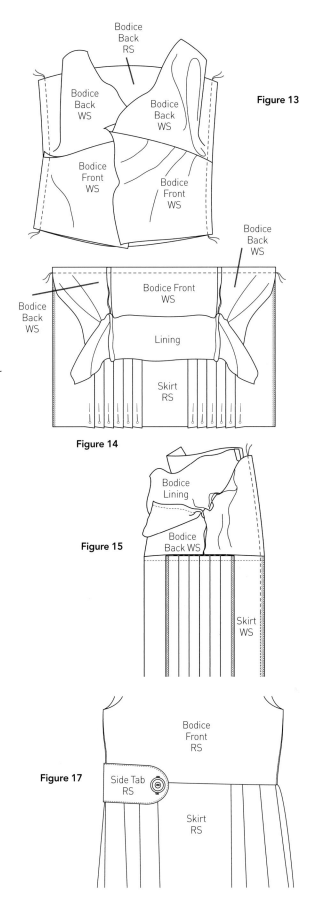

Figure 13

Figure 14

Figure 15

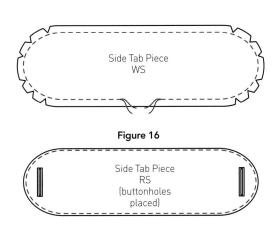

Figure 16

Figure 17

Fairlane dress

Airy layers of fabric and a high/low hem set this dress apart. Fold-over elastic straps and an elastic waist keep it comfortable while the silhouette makes it unique. Use a mesh or chiffon fabric and lining for an ombré effect.

Materials

FABRIC
Shown: Nylon mesh knit (outer) and polyester matte jersey (lining) (See chart on next page for amounts)

NOTIONS
3 yd (2.7m) of fold-over elastic

1" (2.6cm) wide elastic: 1 yd (0.9m) for dress sizes 0–12, or 1¼ yd (1.1m) for dress sizes 14–22

NOTES
If your fabric isn't sheer, you can skip the lining for this dress.

½" (1.3cm) seams used unless otherwise noted.

Refer to Chapter 1 for basic sewing techniques and information on customizing fit.

Front

Back

Fairlane Dress

1. Trace off the front and back bodice pieces.

2. Modify the front bodice (**Figure 1**).

   a. Make a mark (A) 2" (5.1cm) down from the neckline.

   b. Make a mark (B) at the midpoint of the shoulder.

   c. Draw a line (C) between marks A and B.

   d. Measure in ¾" (1.9cm) from the shoulder on line C and make a mark (D).

   e. Draw a new armhole curve line (E) from mark D to the armscye.

   f. Measure the original neckline as indicated on Figure 1 and make a note of that measurement. Original front neckline measurement: _____

   g. Cut through the center of the bust dart to the bust point. Cut from the neckline parallel to the center front to the bust point. Rotate the bust dart closed, opening a neckline dart. Tape the bust dart closed and add paper under the neckline area. True up the new front neckline, drawing a straight line from mark D to mark A.

3. Modify the back bodice (**Figure 2**).

   a. Make a mark (A) 2" (5.1cm) down from the neckline.

   b. Make a mark (B) at the midpoint of the shoulder.

   c. From mark B, measure in ¾" (1.9cm) at a 90° angle to the shoulder seam and make another mark (C).

   d. Draw a slightly curved line (D) between marks A and C.

   e. Draw a line (E) from mark C to the armscye.

Fabric Needs

Dress Size	If using 44/45" (111.8/114.3cm) fabric, in yards (meters)				If using 58/60" (147.3/152.4cm) fabric, in yards (meters)			
	Top Tier	Middle tier	Bottom tier	Lining	Top tier	Middle tier	Bottom tier	Lining
0	1¾ yd (1.6m)	1½ yd (1.4m)	2 yd (1.8m)	2¾ yd (2.5m)	1½ yd (1.4m)	¾ yd (0.7m)	1 yd (0.9m)	2¾ yd (2.5m)
2	1¾ yd (1.6m)	1½ yd (1.4m)	2 yd (1.8m)	2¾ yd (2.5m)	1½ yd (1.4m)	¾ yd (0.7m)	1 yd (0.9m)	2¾ yd (2.5m)
4	1¾ yd (1.6m)	1½ yd (1.4m)	2 yd (1.8m)	2¾ yd (2.5m)	1½ yd (1.4m)	¾ yd (0.7m)	1 yd (0.9m)	2¾ yd (2.5m)
6	1¾ yd (1.6m)	1½ yd (1.4m)	2 yd (1.8m)	2¾ yd (2.5m)	1½ yd (1.4m)	¾ yd (0.7m)	1 yd (0.9m)	2¾ yd (2.5m)
8	1¾ yd (1.6m)	1½ yd (1.4m)	2 yd (1.8m)	2¾ yd (2.5m)	1¾ yd (1.6m)	1½ yd (1.4m)	2 yd (1.8m)	2¾ yd (2.5m)
10	1¾ yd (1.6m)	1½ yd (1.4m)	2 yd (1.8m)	2¾ yd (2.5m)	1¾ yd (1.6m)	1½ yd (1.4m)	2 yd (1.8m)	2¾ yd (2.5m)
12	1¾ yd (1.6m)	1½ yd (1.4m)	2 yd (1.8m)	2¾ yd (2.5m)	1¾ yd (1.6m)	1½ yd (1.4m)	2 yd (1.8m)	2¾ yd (2.5m)
14	2⅓ yd (2.1m)	1½ yd (1.4m)	2 yd (1.8m)	3½ yd (3.2m)	2⅓ yd (2.1m)	1½ yd (1.4m)	2 yd (1.8m)	2¾ yd (2.5m)
16	2⅓ yd (2.1m)	1½ yd (1.4m)	2 yd (1.8m)	3½ yd (3.2m)	2⅓ yd (2.1m)	1½ yd (1.4m)	2 yd (1.8m)	2¾ yd (2.5m)
18	2⅓ yd (2.1m)	1½ yd (1.4m)	2 yd (1.8m)	3½ yd (3.2m)	2⅓ yd (2.1m)	1½ yd (1.4m)	2 yd (1.8m)	2¾ yd (2.5m)
20	2⅓ yd (2.1m)	1⅝ yd (1.5m)	2 yd (1.8m)	3½ yd (3.2m)	2⅓ yd (2.1m)	1⅝ yd (1.5m)	2 yd (1.8m)	2¾ yd (2.5m)
22	2⅓ yd (2.1m)	1⅝ yd (1.5m)	2 yd (1.8m)	3½ yd (3.2m)	2⅓ yd (2.1m)	1⅝ yd (1.5m)	2 yd (1.8m)	2¾ yd (2.5m)

f. Measure the original neckline as indicated on Figure 2 and make a note of that measurement. Original back neckline measurement:

_____

g. Add 1" (2.6cm) to the center back of the bodice.

4. Cut out the new front and back pattern pieces (**Figure 3**). Then, cut both bodice pattern pieces on the fold out of main fabric; these will be strapless. Disregard the waist darts. If using sheer fabric, cut both bodice patterns out of lining as well.

5. Measure the front and back armscye, and add these numbers together. Cut two fold-over elastic straps this length.

6. Add the measurements for the original front and back neckline together and multiply this number by 2. Add 3" (7.6cm) to that number and cut a piece of fold-over elastic to that length. If needed, you can piece two lengths of fold-over elastic together for this piece by zigzag stitching two short ends together.

7. For the top skirt, cut a rectangle 2 times the waist measurement in width, and 7" (17.8cm) shorter than knee length (see the skirt measurement guide in Chapter 1). For the middle skirt, cut the same width but knee length. For the bottom skirt, cut the same width but midi length. If your fabric is sheer, cut the bottom skirt out of lining as well. If you need to piece panels for any skirt layer, cut two, each the same width as the waist measurement plus 1" (2.6cm). Then sew the two skirt panels right sides together.

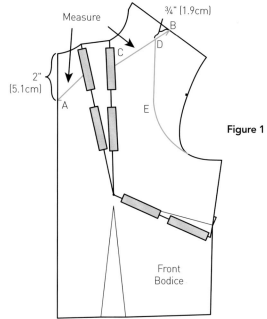

Figure 1

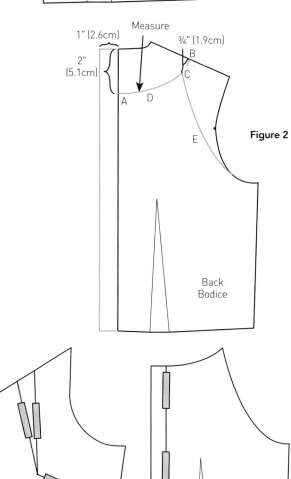

Figure 2

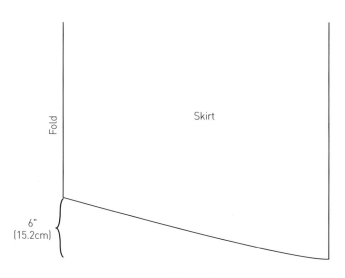

Figure 4

Figure 3

8. Fold each skirt piece in half, matching the side seam edges. Mark each skirt 6" (15.2cm) up from the bottom on the center front. Draw a diagonal line from this to the center back and cut along this line (Figure 4).

9. If you have not already pieced the skirt panels together, fold each skirt piece right sides together, then stitch down and finish the center back seam.

10. If needed, hem the bottom edge of each skirt by folding ¼" (6mm) to the wrong side twice and stitching to form a narrow hem. *Note:* The dress shown was made from knit fabric, which does not unravel along the edges like woven fabric does, so it was left unhemmed.

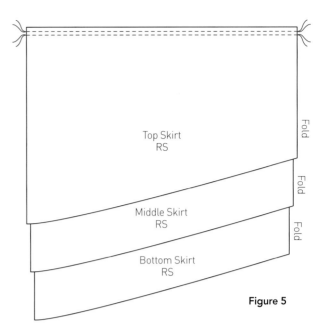

Figure 5

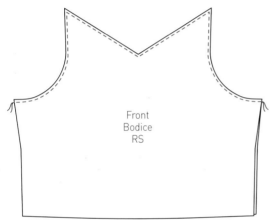

Figure 6

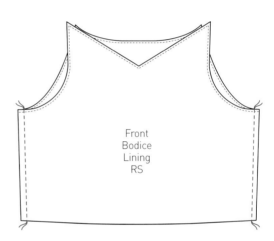

Figure 7

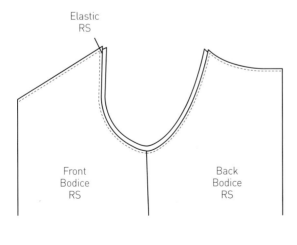

Figure 8

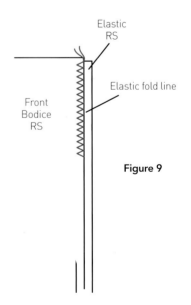

Figure 9

11. Layer the three skirt pieces over each other, wrong side of the top skirt to right side of the middle skirt, wrong side of the middle skirt to right side of the bottom skirt. If using lining, put that layer underneath all of them. Match the seams. Baste skirts together along the waistline edge with gathering stitches (Figure 5). Set aside.

12. If using lining, baste lining pieces wrong sides together with the front and back bodice pieces (Figure 6).

13. Sew the front bodice to the back bodice at the side seams (Figure 7). Finish these seams.

14. Fold the bodice to work on one armscye. Pin the fold-over elastic wrong sides together with the armscye, matching the fold line on the elastic with the raw edge of the fabric. Stitch the elastic in place, using a narrow zigzag stitch (Figures 8–10).

15. Fold the elastic to the right side of the bodice. Stitch in place close to the edge, using a narrow zigzag stitch (Figure 11).

16. Repeat steps 14–15 with the other armscye.

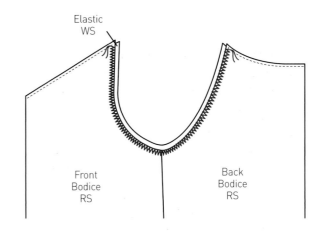

Figure 10

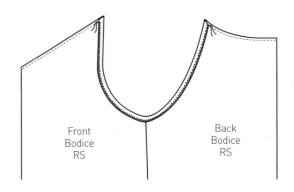

Figure 11

Figure 12

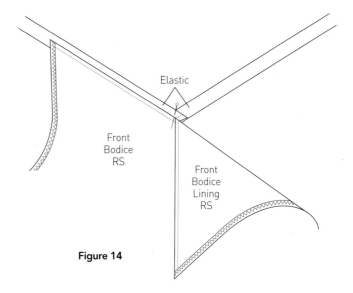

Figure 13

17. Fold the neckline fold-over elastic in half and mark the center on the wrong side—this is the center back. Measure to each side of this mark the amount of the original back neckline measurement and make two more marks—these are the start of the straps. Measure 1½" (3.8cm) from each of these marks and make two final marks—these are the ends of the straps. The remaining elastic on each end will be for the front neckline (Figure 12).

18. Cut the two short ends of the elastic in a V-shape with the point ½" (1.3cm) in from the short edge and at the fold line. Stitch the V-shape (Figure 13).

Figure 14

19. Place the V of the elastic with the stitched point aligned with the bodice center front, wrong sides together. Pin the point of the neckline (**Figure 14**).

20. Line up the strap marks with the edges of the front bodice and pin. Then line up the other strap marks with the back edges of the back bodice and the center back mark with the center back of the bodice. Pin each point. Stitch the elastic to the bodice, stretching the elastic flat so it matches the neckline and using a narrow zigzag stitch (**Figure 15**).

21. Fold the elastic to the right side of the bodice. Stitch in place close to the edge, using a narrow zigzag stitch (**Figure 16**).

22. Gather the skirt to match the width of the bodice, matching center front and center back (**Figure 17**).

23. Place the skirt and bodice right sides together, matching the waistline, and stitch.

24. Cut the 1" (2.6cm) elastic to the same length as the waist measurement. Overlap short ends and stitch with a zigzag stitch to form a loop (**Figure 18**). Mark quarter points on the elastic loop.

25. With the dress wrong-side out and the bodice around the skirt, place the elastic loop around the waist and match the elastic with raw fabric edges. Match the marks on the elastic with the center front, center back, and bodice side seams and pin. Stitch down the center of the elastic with a zigzag stitch, stretching the elastic flat to the fabric as you stitch (**Figure 19**). If desired you can also stitch the elastic to the skirt at each edge. Pay attention to your bobbin thread for this step, as it will show on the front of the dress.

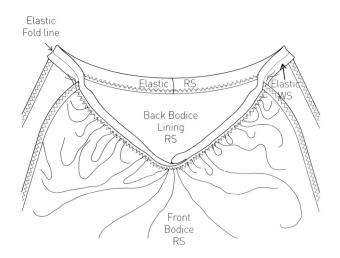

Figure 15

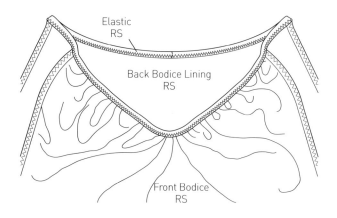

Figure 16

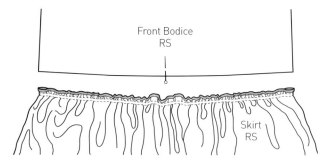

Figure 17

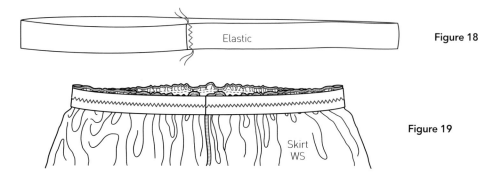

Figure 18

Figure 19

4

Al Fresco

One of the best parts of summer is spending time outdoors. Whether you're at a picnic lunch or enjoying an evening on the patio, these dresses fit the bill.

Pennybacker dress

Named after a soaring Austin bridge, this dress whispers of summer days spent at the lake, picnicking, swimming and barbecuing. The drawstring waist lets you pull it over a swimsuit, while the double ruffled skirt adds just the right touch of sweetness.

Front

Back

Materials

FABRIC
Shown: Dotted Swiss

Dress Size	44/45" (111.8/114.3cm)	or	58/60" (147.3/152.4cm)
0	5½ yd (5m)		4 yd (3.7m)
2	5½ yd (5m)		4 yd (3.7m)
4	5½ yd (5m)		4 yd (3.7m)
6	5½ yd (5m)		4 yd (3.7m)
8	5½ yd (5m)		4 yd (3.7m)
10	5½ yd (5m)		5½ yd (5m)
12	5½ yd (5m)	or	5½ yd (5m)
14	7 yd (6.4m)		5½ yd (5m)
16	7 yd (6.4m)		5½ yd (5m)
18	7 yd (6.4m)		5½ yd (5m)
20	7 yd (6.4m)		5½ yd (5m)
22	7 yd (6.4m)		5½ yd (5m)

NOTIONS
1 package extra-wide double-fold bias tape

½" (1.3cm) wide elastic, the same length as your waist measurement

NOTES
Fabric amounts listed include enough for lining in the same fabric. Recalculate if using different material for lining.

½" (1.3cm) seams used unless otherwise noted.

Refer to Chapter 1 for basic sewing techniques and information on customizing fit.

Pennybacker Dress

1. Trace off the front and back bodice pieces.

2. Modify the front bodice (**Figure 1**).

   a. Make a mark (A) 2¾" (7cm) down from the center front neck.

   b. Make a mark (B) 2" (5.1cm) in from the neck edge of the shoulder.

   c. Draw a curve (C) to connect marks A and B; cut pattern along this curve.

   d. Cut through the center line of the bust dart almost to the bust point.

   e. Cut through the center line of the waist dart almost to the bust point.

   f. Rotate the pattern piece so that the bust dart legs lie over one another. Tape this dart closed, increasing the size of the waist dart. Fold the extra flaps on the bust dart into the side seam.

   g. Draw a curved waistline connecting the waist dart legs, then omit the dart. Cut one front bodice on the fold out of main fabric, and one on the fold out of lining fabric (**Figure 2**).

3. Modify the back bodice.

   a. Cut ½" (1.3cm) off the center back line (this is a seam allowance included for the zipper but this dress does not have a zipper).

   b. Make a mark (A) 2½" (6.4cm) down from the center back neck (**Figure 3**).

   c. Make a mark (B) 2" (5.1cm) in from the neck edge of the shoulder seam (**Figure 3**).

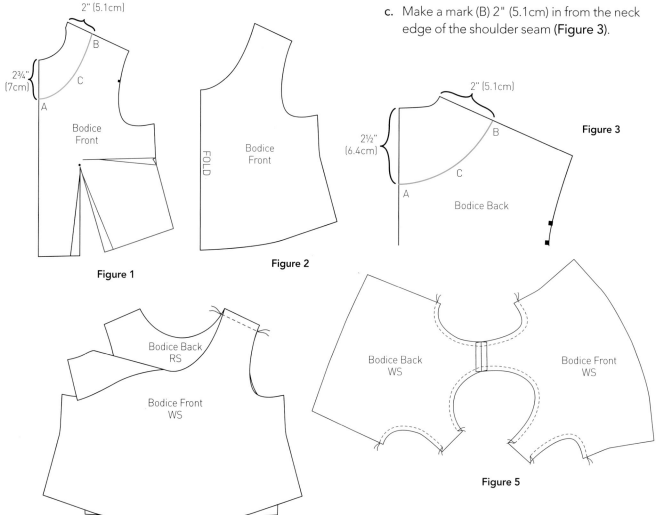

Figure 1

Figure 2

Figure 3

Figure 4

Figure 5

d. Draw a curve (C) connecting marks A and B. Cut pattern along this curve (Figure 3).

e. Omit the waist dart as done on the front bodice.

f. Cut one back bodice with the center back placed on the fold out of main fabric. Cut one back bodice with the center back placed on the fold out of lining fabric.

4. Cut skirt. Refer to the skirt measurement guide in Chapter 1 to cut a rectangular gathered skirt. Skirt shown is knee length minus 3" (7.6cm) and 2 times the waist measurement in width.

5. Cut overskirt. Overskirt shown is 1" (2.5cm) shorter than the skirt and the same width.

6. Cut ruffles. Skirt ruffle is 4½" (11.4cm) tall and 2 times the skirt width (you will need to cut multiple pieces to get the correct length). Overskirt ruffle is 3½" (8.9cm) tall and 2 times the skirt width (you may need to cut multiple pieces).

7. Cut two drawstrings 1½" (3.8cm) wide by 22" (55.9cm) long. Cut a piece of ½" (1.3cm) wide elastic long enough that when added to the two drawstring pieces, the total length is 2 times the waist measurement.

8. Place front and back bodice pieces right sides together and sew the left shoulder (Figure 4). Place the front and back lining right sides together and sew the right shoulder.

9. Place bodice and lining right sides together. Stitch together around the armholes and neckline, starting and stopping ½" (1.3cm) away from the shoulder edge on the shoulder raw edges (Figure 5). Clip curves of armhole, to but not through the stitching. Turn the bodice right-side out.

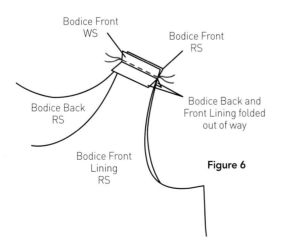

Bodice Front
WS

Bodice Front
RS

Bodice Back
RS

Bodice Back and
Front Lining folded
out of way

Bodice Front
Lining
RS

Figure 6

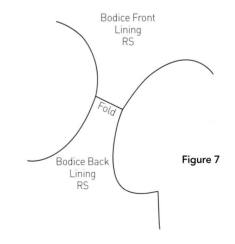

Bodice Front
Lining
RS

Fold

Bodice Back
Lining
RS

Figure 7

10. Fold bodice right sides together. Sew the open shoulder edges of the main fabric together (**Figure 6**).

11. Fold one of the raw edges of the shoulder lining ½" (1.3cm) to the inside. Push the other raw edge underneath this folded edge (**Figure 7**). On the right side, stitch in the ditch of the shoulder seam to secure lining in place, or secure with a slipstitch.

12. Pin the side seams of the outer fabric right sides together. Pin the side seams of the lining right sides together. Make sure to match armhole seams. Sew the side seams in one line from main fabric to lining (**Figure 8**).

13. Stitch a ½" (1.3cm) vertical buttonhole at the bodice center front, ¾" (1.9cm) away from the raw waist edge. This will be the exit opening for your drawstring (**Figure 9**).

14. Fold the skirt right sides together, matching short edges. Stitch short edge and finish seam; this is the center back seam. Repeat with overskirt, skirt ruffle and overskirt ruffle.

15. Finish one raw edge of the skirt ruffle by turning ¼" (6mm) to the wrong side twice then stitching to form a narrow hem. Repeat with both long edges of the overskirt ruffle.

16. Gather the remaining raw edge of the skirt ruffle to the same width as the skirt. Pin ruffle to skirt, right sides together, and stitch (**Figure 10**). Finish seam with an overlock stitch or faux overlock stitch.

17. Gather the overskirt ruffle with stitches ½" (1.3cm) from one hemmed edge to the same width as the overskirt. Place the overskirt ruffle wrong side against the overskirt right side and stitch in place over the gathering stitches (**Figure 11**).

18. Place the skirt inside the overskirt, both right-side out, matching top edges and center back seams. Gather top edges to match width of bodice at waistline; basting stitches for gathering should be sewn through both layers at the same time.

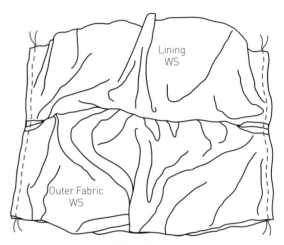

Figure 8

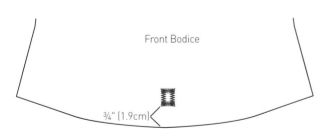

Figure 9

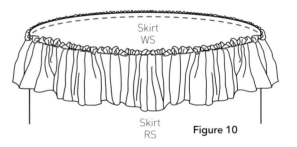

Figure 10

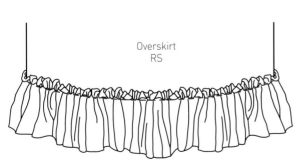

Figure 11

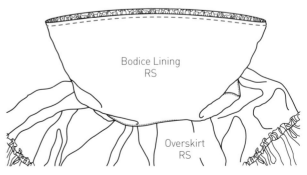

Figure 12

19. Turn bodice lining side out. Put the skirt/overskirt combo inside the bodice, matching waistlines and center back seam. Pin bodice and lining fabric to the skirt combo and stitch through all four layers (**Figure 12**).

20. Turn dress wrong-side out, and place bodice inside skirt. Open up extra-wide double-fold bias tape. Starting at the center back, place the bias tape right side against the skirt wrong side, matching raw edges and pinning around the waistline. Overlap the ends of the bias tape before cutting the tape. Stitch in the fold line closest to the waistline raw edge (**Figure 13**).

21. Press the bias tape up toward the bodice, folding only the top fold to the wrong side to form a 1" (2.6cm) casing. Keeping the bodice fabric is flat, topstitch the bias tape close to the fold (**Figure 14**). Your stitching will show on the right side, so use an appropriate color of bobbin thread.

22. Fold the drawstring pieces right sides together, matching long edges. Stitch with ¼" (6mm) seams. Turn drawstrings right-side out (a tube turner will help). Press with seam along one edge. Place end of elastic inside one raw edge of drawstring tube and stitch across end to secure elastic and close the end of the tube. Repeat with the other end of elastic and one end of the other drawstring.

23. Using a safety pin, thread the drawstring in through the center front buttonhole, around the waistline casing, and back out through the buttonhole. Knot the ends of the drawstring.

Wear this in autumn with long boots and a light jacket; in even cooler weather add leggings, ankle boots, a short or long sleeve slouchy sweatshirt and a belt.

Bodice WS

Bias Tape WS

Figure 13

Center Back

Skirt WS

Bodice WS

Bias Tape RS

Figure 14

Center Back

Skirt WS

Bailey dress

Perfect for playtime or a trip for lemonade, the Bailey Dress features a seamed bodice and skirt with piped accents. Hide summer treasures in the large pockets and add a touch of charm with optional decorative buttons.

Front

Back

Materials

FABRIC
Shown: Quilting weight cotton

Dress Size	Main Fabric 44/45" (111.8/ 114.3cm)		Main Fabric 58/60" (147.3/ 152.4cm)	Contrast Fabric (either width)
2T	1½ yd (1.4m)		1½ yd (1.4m)	¼ yd (0.2m)
3T	1½ yd (1.4m)		1½ yd (1.4m)	¼ yd (0.2m)
4T	1¾ yd (1.6m)		1¾ yd (1.6m)	¼ yd (0.2m)
5	1¾ yd (1.6m)		1¾ yd (1.6m)	¼ yd (0.2m)
6	2 yd (1.8m)	or	2 yd (1.8m)	¼ yd (0.2m)
8	2 yd (1.8m)		2 yd (1.8m)	¼ yd (0.2m)
10	2 yd (1.8m)		2 yd (1.8m)	¼ yd (0.2m)
12	2 yd (1.8m)		2 yd (1.8m)	¼ yd (0.2m)

NOTIONS
Three ½"–⅝" (1.3cm–1.6cm) buttons

2 packages of piping (3 packages for sizes 10 and 12)

14" (35.6cm) zipper

NOTES
Main fabric amounts listed include enough for lining in the same fabric. Recalculate if using different material for lining.

½" (1.3cm) seams used unless otherwise noted.

Refer to Chapter 1 for basic sewing techniques and information on customizing fit.

Bailey Dress

1. Trace off the front and back bodice pieces.

2. Modify the front bodice (**Figure 1**).

   a. Draw a horizontal line (A) at the level of the bottom of the armhole.

   b. Measure vertically between the neckline and line A. Mark a point halfway between the two. Draw a horizontal line (B) at this point for the new neckline.

   c. Mark 2" (5.1cm) from the bottom of the bodice piece, measuring up 2" (5.1cm) from the side (not the center front), and draw a horizontal cutline (C).

   d. Cut the bodice along lines B and C.

   e. Measure the center front of the bodice. Make a center front pattern piece that is this length and 2" (5.1cm) wide (**Figure 2**).

3. Modify the back bodice (**Figure 3**).

   a. Draw a horizontal line (A) at the level of the bottom of the armhole.

   b. Mark 2" (5.1cm) from the bottom of the bodice piece, measuring up from the bottom edge, and draw a horizontal cutline (B).

   c. Cut the back bodice along these two lines.

4. Cut one front bodice pattern piece on the fold out of lining. Cut two more front bodice pieces out of main fabric, mirrored and not on the fold. Cut one center front bodice piece out of main fabric. Cut two back bodice pattern pieces out of main fabric and out of lining (mirrored). Cut two straps 12" (30.5cm) long and 4" (10.2cm) wide.

5. For the skirt, cut one front panel that is half of the waist measurement in width, and knee length (see the skirt measurement guide in Chapter 1). Then cut two side skirt panels that are one-third of the waist width and knee length. Cut two back skirt panels that are one-quarter of the waist width plus 1" (2.6cm) each, and knee length.

6. Cut two pockets that are the same width as the side skirt panels and one-third of the length. *Note:* The hem band will be cut later.

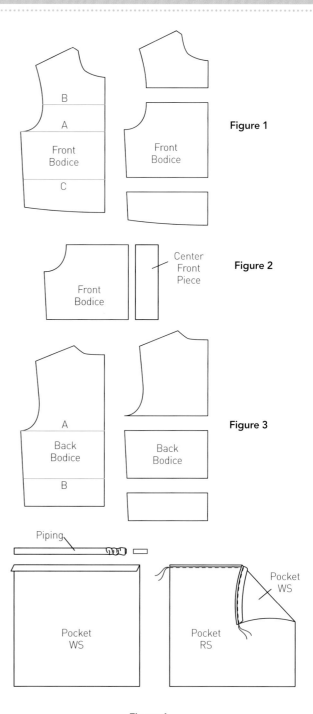

Figure 1

Figure 2

Figure 3

Figure 4

7. Cut two pieces of piping to the same width as the top of the pockets. At each end of the piping, remove ½" (1.3cm) of the cording by pushing back the casing, cutting the cording, then pulling the casing back out. This will keep the cording out of the seam allowances.

11. Cut four pieces of piping the same length as the skirt panels. Remove ½" (1.3cm) from each end of each piece of piping. Place the piping on the left side of one side panel. Place one back panel right sides together with the side panel, matching the left edges and sandwiching the piping. Stitch, using a piping or zipper foot. Finish this seam. Repeat this process with the other side and back panels, sewing the right side seam this time. You should have two side/back panel combos that mirror each other (**Figures 6 and 7**).

12. Place another piece of piping on the open side of one side panel. Place the front skirt panel right sides together with the side panel, matching raw edges. Stitch, using a piping or zipper foot. Finish this seam. Repeat this process with the other side of the front skirt panel.

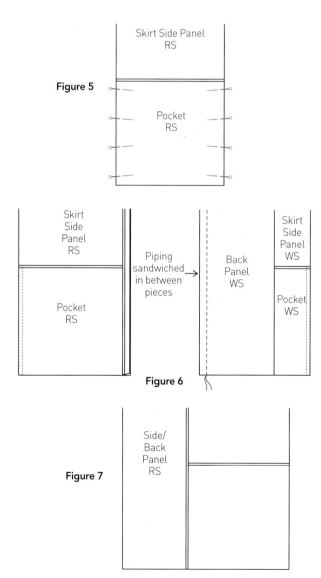

8. Press the top edge of each pocket ¼" (6mm) to the wrong side.

9. Pin the piping to the wrong side of each pocket, with the folded edge of the pocket against the cording. Using a zipper or piping presser foot, topstitch on the right side of the pocket to secure the piping in place (**Figure 4**).

10. Pin a pocket to each skirt side panel, matching the bottom edges of the pockets with the bottom edges of the skirt panels (**Figure 5**). Baste the sides of the pockets in place.

13. Fold the skirt in half, right sides together, matching the center back seam. Measure the length of the back bodice and mark this amount from the top down on the zipper tape. Match the zipper from that mark down on the skirt back seam and mark the skirt fabric just above the zipper stop. Baste the center back seam to the zipper mark, then stop, backstitch, and change to a regular stitch length for the rest of the seam.

14. Mark the center front of the skirt.

15. Cut two pieces of piping the same length as the center front bodice piece. Remove ½" (1.3cm) of each end of each piece of piping. Place the piping along the center front seam of one of the bodice front pieces. Place the center front piece right sides together with this piece, sandwiching the piping in between. Stitch the seam, using a piping or zipper foot (**Figure 8**). Repeat with the other side of the bodice front.

16. Fold straps in half, right sides together, matching long edges. Sew into tubes, then turn. Press straps with seam on one side.

17. Align each strap ¾" (1.9cm) in from the top corner of the bodice front. Baste in place (**Figure 9**).

18. Place the back bodice pieces right sides together and baste the center back seam (**Figure 10**).

19. Pin the bodice front to the bodice back, right sides together, matching the side seams. Stitch (**Figure 11**). Mark the center front of the bodice. Repeat this step with the bodice linings, though the center back seam of the lining is not sewn.

20. Gather the skirt to the same width as the bodice, matching the center back seams (**Figure 12**). Measure and make sure the side panels each start at the same distance away from the center back seam and from the center front.

21. Place the bodice and skirt right sides together, aligning the waist edges and matching the center back seams and center front. Stitch.

22. Insert the zipper in the center back seam (**Figure 13**).

23. Press the bottom edge of the bodice lining ⅜" (1cm) to the wrong side.

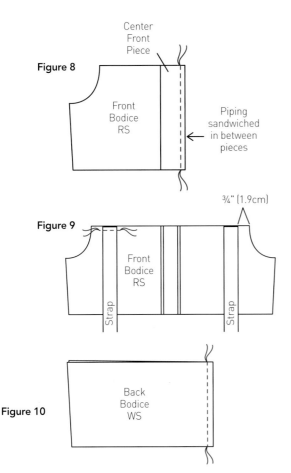

Figure 8

Center Front Piece

Front Bodice RS

Piping sandwiched in between pieces

¾" (1.9cm)

Figure 9

Front Bodice RS

Strap

Strap

Figure 10

Back Bodice WS

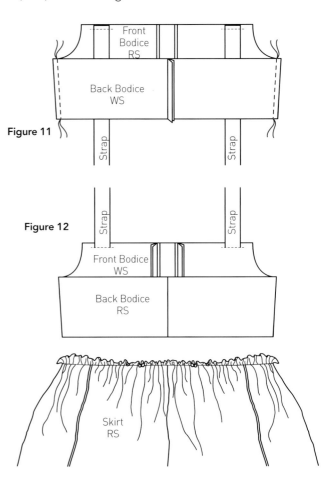

Figure 11

Front Bodice RS

Back Bodice WS

Strap

Strap

Figure 12

Strap

Strap

Front Bodice WS

Back Bodice RS

Skirt RS

24. Unzip the dress. Pin the bodice lining to the bodice around the neckline, right sides together. Lining will extend ½" (1.3cm) past the zipper on each side. Stitch neckline and armholes. Leave openings on back bodice to insert straps; each opening should be above the piping line on the back skirt (**Figure 14**). Stitch lining to bodice. Clip corners.

25. Turn lining to the inside of the dress. Press the edges.

26. Insert the straps into the openings on the back bodice. Adjust to fit (use the original bodice block to adjust length for the size you are sewing). Topstitch the neckline edge to secure the straps.

27. Pin the folded edge of the lining over the waistline seam. On the right side of the dress, stitch in the ditch of the waistline seam to secure the lining, or secure with a slipstitch.

28. Measure around the skirt bottom and add 1" (2.6cm) for the seam allowance and cut a band this measurement by 8" (20.3cm) deep out of contrast fabric. Fold right sides together, matching short ends, and stitch with a ½" (1.3cm) seam allowance.

29. Press one edge of the hem band ⅜" (1cm) to the wrong side.

30. Place the hem band right sides together with the bottom of the skirt, matching raw, unpressed edges and matching the hem band seam with the center back seam. Stitch (**Figure 15**). Press this seam toward the band.

31. Fold the hem band to the wrong side, covering the seam from the previous step with the folded edge. Stitch on the right side of the hem band in the ditch of the seam, to secure hem band in place (**Figure 16**).

32. Stitch buttons onto center front bodice if desired.

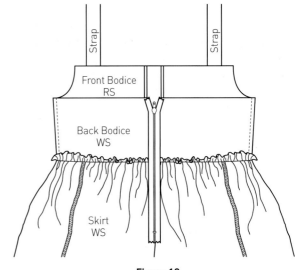

Figure 13

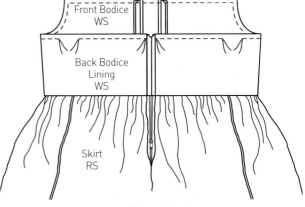

Figure 14

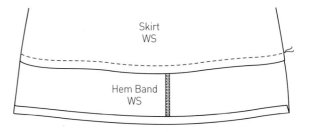

Figure 15

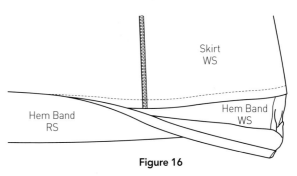

Figure 16

Sutton dress

A neckline that works on or off the shoulder gives options for the dog days of summer. Made in a floaty fabric, this dress can catch the slightest breeze stirring the warm air.

Front

Back

Materials

FABRIC
Shown: Cotton gauze

Dress Size	44/45" (111.8/114.3cm)	or	58/60" (147.3/152.4cm)
0	3 yd (2.7m)		3 yd (2.7m)
2	3 yd (2.7m)		3 yd (2.7m)
4	3 yd (2.7m)		3 yd (2.7m)
6	3 yd (2.7m)		3 yd (2.7m)
8	4 yd (3.7m)		3 yd (2.7m)
10	4 yd (3.7m)		3 yd (2.7m)
12	4 yd (3.7m)	or	3 yd (2.7m)
14	4⅓ yd (4m)		3 yd (2.7m)
16	4⅓ yd (4m)		3 yd (2.7m)
18	4⅓ yd (4m)		3 yd (2.7m)
20	4⅓ yd (4m)		4 yd (3.7m)
22	4⅓ yd (4m)		4 yd (3.7m)

NOTIONS
3 yd (2.7m) of ⅜" (1cm) wide elastic

1 package of single-fold bias tape

NOTES
½" (1.3cm) seams used unless otherwise noted.

Refer to Chapter 1 for basic sewing techniques and information on customizing fit.

Sutton Dress

1. Trace off the front and back bodice pieces.

2. Modify the front bodice (**Figure 1**).

   a. Make a mark (A) 2½" (6.4cm) down on the center front neckline.

   b. Extend the center line (B) of the waist dart up through the bust point and about 5" (12.7cm) beyond.

   c. Draw a horizontal line from mark A to line B that curves down toward the armscye after reaching line B.

   d. Add a ¼" (6mm) casing allowance along the new neckline.

   e. Cut out the new bodice shape, then cut down line B to the bust point. Pivot this piece until the dart legs are on top of each other, to transfer the bust dart fullness to the neckline (**Figure 2**).

   f. Paper over the dart created on the neckline (**Figure 3**).

   g. Slash the entire pattern along the center of the waist dart and spread pieces ½" (1.3cm) apart. Paper over the gap (**Figure 4**).

3. Modify the back bodice.

   a. Draw a line (A) from the point of the armscye to the center back, touching the top point of the back dart. Add a ¼" (6mm) casing allowance along the new neckline (**Figure 5**).

   b. Slash the entire pattern along the center of the waist dart and spread pieces ½" (1.3cm) apart. Paper over the gap (**Figure 6**).

4. Cut front and back bodice pattern pieces on the fold out of main fabric.

5. For the skirt, cut two rectangles to midi skirt length (see the skirt measurement guide in Chapter 1) and 1.5 times the waist measurement in width. You may need to piece three pieces together for larger sizes to get the correct width.

6. For the ruffle, cut two rectangles of fabric that are 7½" (19.1cm) tall and the same width as the elastic length listed in the following chart.

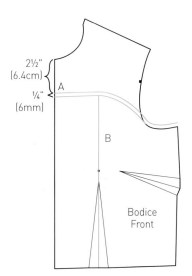

2½"
(6.4cm)

¼"
(6mm)

A

B

Bodice
Front

Figure 1

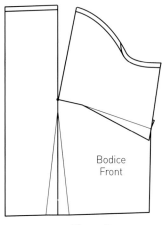

Bodice
Front

Figure 2

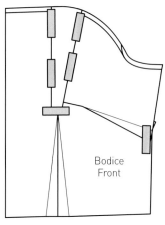

Bodice
Front

Figure 3

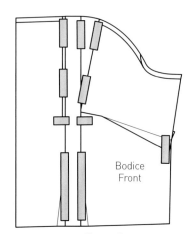

Bodice
Front

Figure 4

SHOULDER ELASTIC CHART	
Dress Size	Elastic Length
0	37½" (95.3cm)
2	38" (96.5cm)
4	38½" (97.8cm)
6	39" (99.1cm)
8	39½" (100.3cm)
10	40" (101.6cm)
12	40½" (102.9cm)
14	41" (104.1cm)
16	42" (106.7cm)
18	43" (109.2cm)
20	44" (111.8cm)
22	45" (114.3cm)

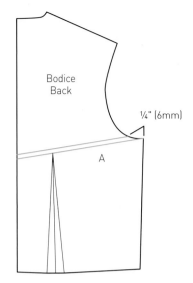

Figure 5

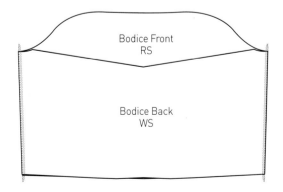

Figure 6

7. Place the ruffle pieces right sides together. Stitch at the side seams. Finish these seams.

8. Fold the bottom edge of the ruffle ¼" (6mm) to the wrong side twice. Stitch, forming a narrow hem.

9. Fold the top edge of the ruffle ¼" (6mm) to the wrong side and press. Fold again, ½" (1.3cm) to the wrong side to form a narrow casing. Stitch, leaving an opening to insert elastic.

10. Cut a piece of ⅜" (1cm) wide elastic to the length on the elastic chart. Use a safety pin to insert it in the ruffle casing, being careful not to twist it.

11. Overlap the edges of the elastic ½" (1.3cm) and stitch together.

12. Sew the opening in the casing closed (**Figure 7**).

13. Place front and back bodice pieces right sides together. Stitch at the side seams. Finish these seams (**Figure 8**).

14. Pin an unfolded piece of single-fold bias tape all around the neckline of the bodice, right sides together, starting at the center back. Fold the short ends of the bias tape ¼" (6mm) to the wrong side at the beginning and end. Stitch along the crease line closest to the edge (**Figure 9**), then turn bias tape to the wrong side of the bodice.

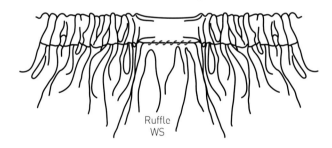

Figure 7

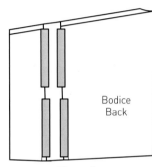

Figure 8

15. Stitch bias tape again along folded edge to form a casing (**Figure 10**).

16. Cut a piece of ⅜" (1cm) wide elastic to the high bust measurement. Using a safety pin, insert elastic in casing starting at center back, being careful not to twist (**Figure 11**).

17. Overlap the edges of the elastic ½" (1.3cm) and stitch together. Stitch down the short edges of the bias tape, anchoring the elastic at center back.

18. Place the skirt pieces right sides together. Stitch at the side seams. Finish these seams.

19. Turn the bottom edge of the skirt ½" (1.3cm) to the wrong side twice to form the hem. Stitch hem.

20. Gather the skirt to the same width as the bottom of the bodice (**Figure 12**).

21. Turn bodice wrong-side out. Put the skirt right-side out inside the bodice, matching waistline and side seams. Pin bodice to the skirt combo and stitch around the waistline.

22. Turn dress wrong-side out, and place bodice inside skirt. Open up single-fold bias tape. Starting at the center back, place the bias tape right side against the skirt wrong side, matching raw edges and pinning around the waistline. Overlap the ends of the bias tape before cutting the tape. Stitch in the fold line closest to the waistline raw edge.

23. Press the bias tape up toward the bodice to form a ½" (1.3cm) casing. Stitch close to the fold, leaving an opening to insert the elastic. Check frequently while sewing to make sure the bodice fabric is smooth and flat. Your stitching will show on the right side, so use an appropriate color of bobbin thread.

24. Cut a piece of ⅜" (1cm) elastic to the waist measurement. Using a safety pin, insert elastic in casing starting at center back, being careful not to twist.

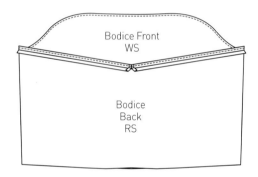

Figure 9

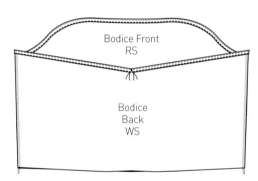

Figure 10

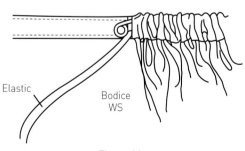

Figure 11

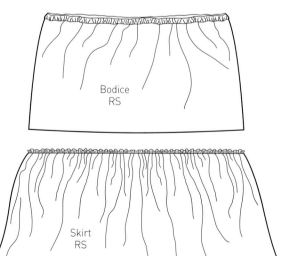

Figure 12

25. Overlap the edges of the elastic ½" (1.3cm) and stitch together. Stitch the opening closed.

26. Place the ruffle over the bodice, wrong side of the ruffle to the right side of the bodice, matching the side seams. Stitch the ruffle to the bodice in a vertical line at the center front and center back, backstitching a few times to make sure it is secure (**Figure 13**). This will prevent sliding inside the casing and leaves the ruffle free to be worn on or off the shoulder.

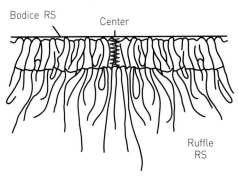

Bodice RS   Center

Ruffle RS

Figure 13

Tarrytown dress

With details like the knotted front straps and shirred back bodice, this dress is both pretty and comfortable for playtime. Try mixing and matching prints for fun looks.

Front

Back

Materials

FABRIC
Shown: Quilting weight cotton

Dress Size	Main Fabric 44/45" (111.8/114.3cm)		Main Fabric 58/60" (147.3/152.4cm)	Contrast Fabric (either width)
2T	1⅛ yd (1m)	or	1 yd (0.9m)	½ yd (0.5m)
3T	1⅛ yd (1m)		1 yd (0.9m)	½ yd (0.5m)
4T	1⅛ yd (1m)		1 yd (0.9m)	½ yd (0.5m)
5	1⅛ yd (1m)		1 yd (0.9m)	½ yd (0.5m)
6	1¾ yd (1.6m)	or	1⅛ yd (1m)	½ yd (0.5m)
8	1¾ yd (1.6m)		1⅛ yd (1m)	½ yd (0.5m)
10	1¾ yd (1.6m)		1⅛ yd (1m)	½ yd (0.5m)
12	1¾ yd (1.6m)		1⅛ yd (1m)	½ yd (0.5m)

NOTIONS
Elastic thread

NOTES
½" (1.3cm) seams used unless otherwise noted.

Refer to Chapter 1 for basic sewing techniques and information on customizing fit.

Tarrytown Dress

1. Trace off the front bodice piece.

2. Modify the front bodice (**Figure 1**).

   a. Draw a horizontal line (A) at the level of the bottom of the armhole.

   b. Measure vertically between the neckline and line A. Mark a point (B) one-quarter of the way down from the neckline.

   c. Draw a curved line (C) from this point to the armscye.

3. Draw the dress back.

   a. Measure the width (D) of the front bodice piece (**Figure 2a**).

   b. Measure the length (E) of the bodice piece (**Figure 2a**) from the point of the armscye to the waist.

   c. Draw a rectangle where the width is measurement D times 1.75, and the length is measurement E plus the knee-length skirt measurement (see the skirt measurement guide in Chapter 1). You should have one large rectangle, 1.75 times the width of the bodice, and the length of the bodice plus the length of the skirt (**Figure 2b**).

4. Cut two of the front bodice piece on the fold out of main fabric.

5. Cut the back dress piece on the fold out of main fabric. Mark the line that was the bottom of the bodice length on the right side.

6. Cut the front skirt panel to 1.75 times the waist measurement in width, and knee length.

7. Measure the width of the dress back and the width of the skirt front panel. Add these two measurements and then subtract 1" (2.6cm). Cut the hem band to that length and 7" (17.8cm) wide.

8. Cut two straps that are 5" (12.7cm) wide and the appropriate length from the chart below.

Dress Size	Elastic Length
2T	16" (40.6cm)
3T	16½" (41.9cm)
4T	17" (43.2cm)
5	17½" (44.5cm)
6	18" (45.7cm)
8	19" (48.3cm)
10	20" (50.8cm)
12	21" (53.3cm)

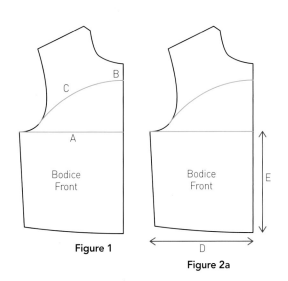

Figure 1

Figure 2a

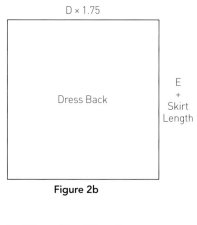

D × 1.75

Dress Back

E + Skirt Length

Figure 2b

Figure 3

Strap WS

Fold

9. Fold the straps in half, right sides together, matching long edges. Cut one short edge of each strap in a rounded curve (**Figure 3**).

10. Stitch long and curved edges of the straps, clip curves, then turn the straps right-side out. Press, turning raw edges ½" (1.3cm) to the inside of the tubes.

11. Take one bodice piece and press the bottom and side edges ⅜" (1cm) to the wrong side. This will be the inner bodice piece.

12. Place the two bodice front pieces right sides together, unfolding the side edges of the inner bodice. Stitch along the top curved edge (**Figure 4**). Clip curves, turn right-side out and press.

13. Gather the front skirt panel to the same width as the front bodice.

Figure 4

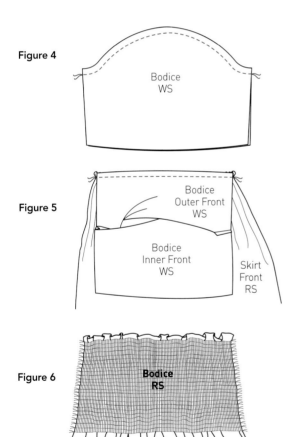

Figure 5

Figure 6

14. Pin the outer front bodice to the front skirt, right sides together, matching waist seams. Stitch (**Figure 5**).

15. Fold the top edge of the dress back ¼" (6mm) to the wrong side twice to form a narrow hem. Stitch.

16. Starting ½" (1.3cm) above the marked line that indicates the bottom of the bodice, shirr the dress back using elastic thread. Continue to shirr, with stitching lines ¼" (6mm) apart, moving toward the top of the dress back. Finish ½" (1.3cm) from the top of the dress back (**Figure 6**).

17. Place the dress back and the dress front right sides together. Match the top of the dress back with the seam joining the outer to inner bodice. Pin down the side seams. Stitch and finish side seams, pressing seams toward the dress front (**Figure 7**).

18. Fold the inner bodice to the inside of the dress. Cover the waist seam with the pressed edge of the inner bodice. Cover the side seams with the sides of the inner bodice piece (**Figure 8**). Stitch in the ditch of the front waistline and side seams to secure the inner bodice piece.

19. Fold the hem band in half, matching short edges. Stitch.

20. Press one edge of the hem band ⅜" (1cm) to the wrong side.

21. Place the hem band right sides together with the bottom of the skirt, matching raw, unpressed edges and matching the hem band seam with a side seam. Stitch (**Figure 9**). Press this seam toward the band.

22. Fold the hem band to the wrong side, covering the seam from the previous step with the folded edge. Stitch on the right side of the hem band in the ditch of the seam, to secure hem band in place (**Figure 10**).

23. Make a 1" (2.6cm) long vertical buttonhole in the center front of the bodice, ½" (1.3cm) from the top edge (**Figure 11**).

24. Sew the uncurved short edges of the straps to the bodice back, approximately 1" (2.6cm) from the side seams and at a very slight angle (**Figure 12**).

25. Pull the straps over the shoulders and through the front bodice buttonhole, then tie in a knot to secure dress (**Figure 13**).

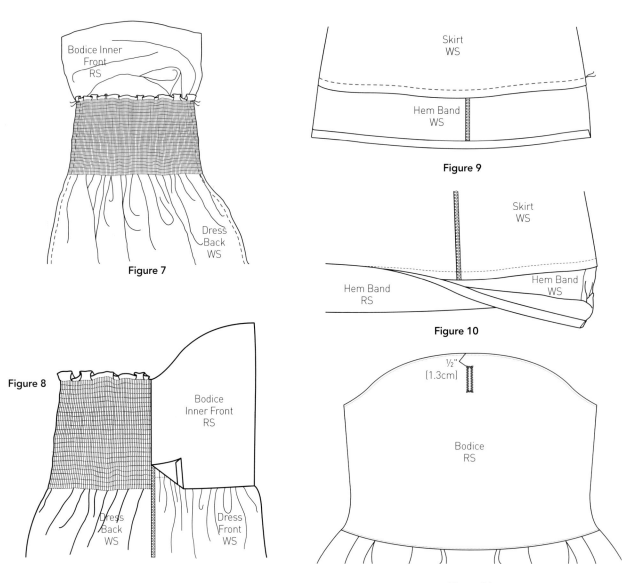

Figure 7

Figure 8

Figure 9

Figure 10

Figure 11

Figure 12

Strap

Strap

Dress
Back
RS

Figure 13

Dress
Front
RS

Bellevue dress

The braided detail on the neckline of this dress is the perfect bohemian touch. The gathered and loose-fitting shape has an airy feel and looks great in both midi and maxi lengths. Use knit fabric for a look like the dress pictured, or woven fabric for a frayed and shabby chic neckline.

Front

Back

Materials

FABRIC
Shown: Nylon mesh knit (for dress and braided trim) backed with polyester matte jersey*

Dress Size	44/45" (111.8/114.3cm)	or	58/60" (147.3/152.4cm)
2T	1⅔ yd (1.5m)		1⅔ yd (1.5m)
3T	1⅔ yd (1.5m)		1⅔ yd (1.5m)
4T	1⅔ yd (1.5m)		1⅔ yd (1.5m)
5	1⅔ yd (1.5m)		1⅔ yd (1.5m)
6	1⅔ yd (1.5m)	or	1⅔ yd (1.5m)
8	1⅔ yd (1.5m)		1⅔ yd (1.5m)
10	1⅔ yd (1.5m)		1⅔ yd (1.5m)
12	1⅔ yd (1.5m)		1⅔ yd (1.5m)

NOTIONS
1 package single-fold bias tape

NOTES
½" (1.3cm) seams used unless otherwise noted.

Refer to Chapter 1 for basic sewing techniques and information on customizing fit.

*For the dress shown, the fabrics together were treated as one piece. To replicate this look, buy the listed yardage amount in both a sheer and a non-sheer fabric.

Bellevue Dress

1. Trace off the front and back bodice pieces.

2. Modify the front bodice.

   a. Draw a horizontal line (A) at the level of the bottom of the armhole (**Figure 1**).

   b. Measure vertically between the point of the neckline and line A. Make a mark (B) half of the way down from the neckline (**Figure 1**).

   c. Draw a horizontal line (C) at the level of the neckline to the armhole. Measure this line, and make a mark (D) at the midpoint (**Figure 1**).

   d. Draw a line (E) from mark B to mark D (**Figure 1**).

   e. Draw a line (F) from mark D to the armscye (**Figure 1**).

   f. Measure the neckline and armhole and note those measurements (**Figure 2**).

   (1) Front neckline measurement: _____

   (2) Front armhole measurement: _____

   g. Make six equally spaced marks along the neckline (**Figure 2**).

   h. Make six equally spaced marks along the waistline. Connect the marks from the neckline to the waistline; these will be at a slight diagonal (**Figure 2**).

   i. Cut the bodice along these lines and number the pieces 1 to 7, starting from the center front edge.

   j. On a sheet of paper long enough to accommodate the bodice length plus skirt length (wrapping paper works well) draw a horizontal line, leaving enough room at the top for your bodice and below for your skirt—this will be your waistline. It does not need to be the exact waistline measurement, as it is simply a guide for building the new bodice. Draw a vertical line perpendicular to this line—this is your center front (**Figure 3**). Measure down from the intersection of the waistline and center front lines the length needed for a midi skirt (see skirt measurement guide in Chapter 1) and draw a line parallel to the waistline.

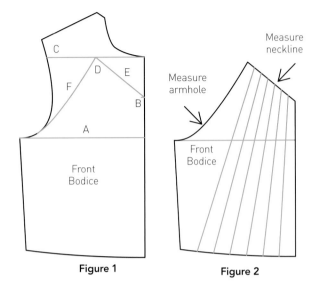

Figure 1

Figure 2

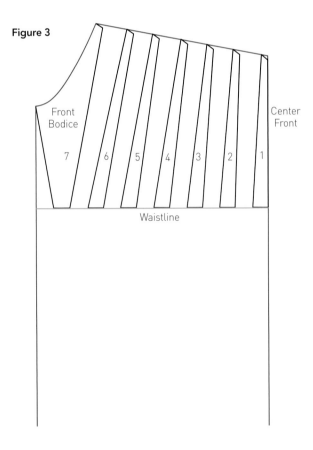

Figure 3

k. Starting with the center front piece of the bodice, tape it to the paper, lining up the center front and waistline. Measure over 1" (2.6cm), then tape the next piece of the bodice, and so on, keeping pieces lined up at the waistline **(Figure 3)**.

l. Draw a vertical line at a 90° angle from the bottom of the armscye and extend to midi length. Draw a straight line down from the center front to the midi length line **(Figure 3)**.

3. Modify the back bodice by repeating steps 2a–l from the front bodice on the back bodice **(Figures 4 and 5)**, EXCEPT change step 2c as follows: Draw the horizontal line at the same level on the armhole as you did on the front bodice, instead of at the neckline. In other words, your line C won't meet the back neckline as it does on the front bodice. To determine where to place line C on the back, measure from line A to C on the center front bodice. Use this measurement to mark the back bodice. For step 2f (to modify back bodice):

   (1) Back neckline measurement: _____

   (2) Back armhole measurement: _____

4. Cut front and back dress pattern pieces; these will be strapless.

5. Cut the front and back dress pieces on the fold out of main fabric.

6. Add the front neckline + front armhole + back neckline + back armhole measurements together. Multiply this total by 2 and then add ½" (1.3cm). Cut a strip of bias tape to this length.

7. Multiply the length of the bias tape strip by 2. Cut three strips of fabric to this length and 2" (5.1cm) wide.

8. Lay your three neckline strips one on top of the other, right sides up. Stitch together across a short edge **(Figure 6)**.

9. Braid the three strips together **(Figures 7–10)**. Stop when the braided strip equals 2 times the front neckline + back neckline. Stitch and trim the strips, laying the three pieces on top of each other and pinning.

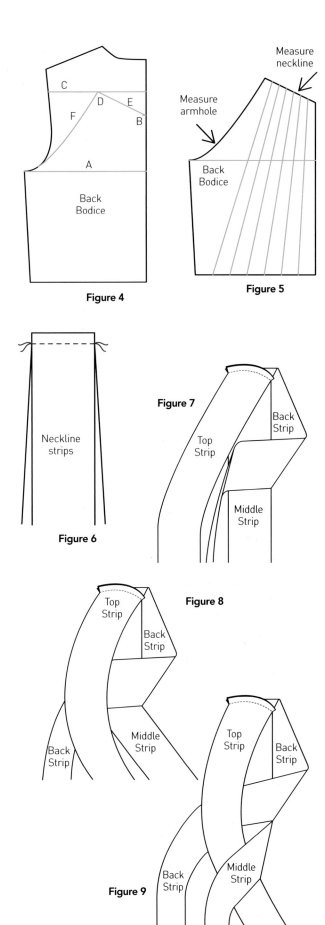

Figure 4

Figure 5

Figure 6

Figure 7

Figure 8

Figure 9

10. Form the braided strip into a circle, placing the ends over the beginning **(Figure 11)**. Stitch through six layers to secure the braid in a circle, and trim the ends of the fabric **(Figure 12)**.

11. Lay out the bias tape strip and measure from one end the front neckline measurement determined in step 2 plus ¼" (6mm) and make a mark. From that point measure a distance equal to the front and back armhole measurements determined in steps 2 and 3. From that mark, measure 2 times the back neckline and make another mark. From that mark, measure the distance equal to the front and back armhole measurements determined in steps 2 and 3 and make another mark. From that point, measure the front neckline measurement determined in step 2 plus ¼" (6mm) and make a final mark. Cut the bias tape strip on this final mark.

12. Lay the front and back dress pieces right sides together and sew the side seams. Finish these seams.

13. Gather the front bodice along the neckline to 2 times the front neckline measurement determined in step 2 (remember, you measured only half the front neckline on the pattern, as it was cut on the fold) **(Figure 13)**.

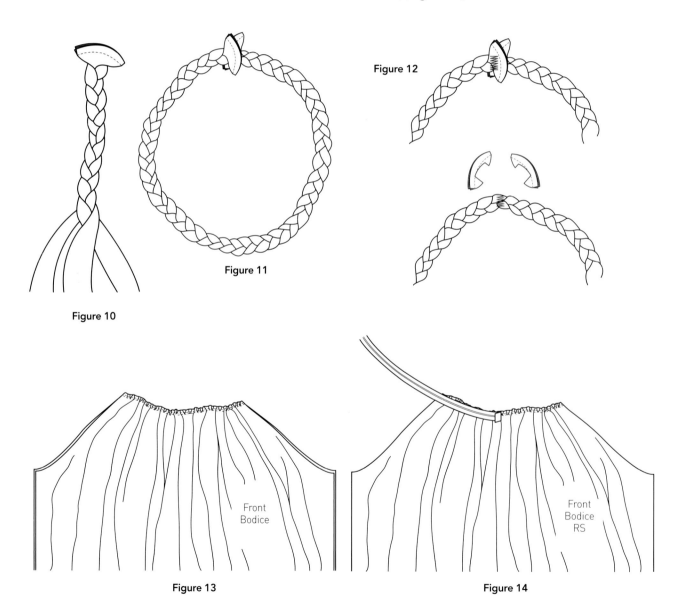

Figure 10

Figure 11

Figure 12

Figure 13

Figure 14

14. Gather the back bodice along the neckline to 2 times the back neckline measurement in step 3.

15. With the dress right-side out, start at the center front and pin the unfolded bias tape right sides together along the neckline, folding the bias tape ¼" (6mm) to the wrong side on the short edge at the center front and matching raw edges. Continue to pin bias tape around the armhole, folding in a tiny miter or tuck at the front points, across the back neckline, adding tiny miters at the points, around the other armhole and around the other half of the front neckline, folding bias tape ¼" (6mm) to the wrong side at the short edge at center front again. Stitch in the crease line closest to the raw edge (**Figures 14 and 15**).

16. Fold bias tape to the wrong side of the dress and pin, allowing the bias tape to fold on the crease lines and pinning. Raw edges should be enclosed under the bias tape. Stitch near the folded edge, being careful to keep gathers from bunching up (**Figure 16**).

17. Mark the center front of the braided neckline band, opposite the stitched part, which is the center back. Match the neckband center front to the dress center front, and the neckband center back to the dress center back. Pin along the right side of the dress front and back, then hand-stitch the neckband in place (**Figure 17**).

17. Hem the dress by turning the bottom edge ½" (1.3cm) to the wrong side twice and stitching.

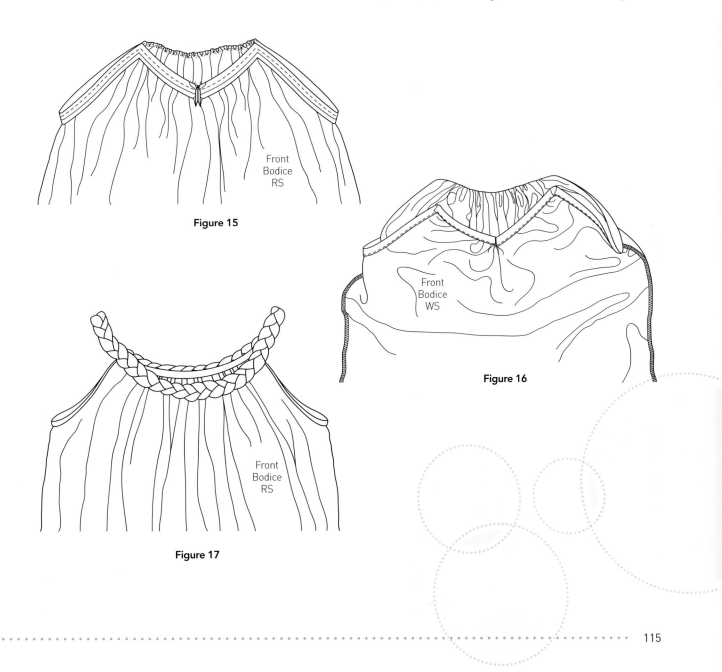

Front Bodice RS

Figure 15

Front Bodice WS

Figure 16

Front Bodice RS

Figure 17

5

Soiree

Special occasions call for special dresses, and the designs in this chapter don't disappoint. Fancy fabrics and delightful details elevate these dresses from everyday wear.

Saltillo dress

Turn up the heat for a summer date night in this piquant maxi dress. Choose fiery sunset colors and keep the party going after the sun goes down.

Materials

FABRIC
Shown: Polyester charmeuse (for bodice) and polyester chiffon (for skirt and ruffle) (See chart on next page for amounts)

NOTIONS
14" (35.6cm) zipper

NOTES
Dress is shown with a coordinating half slip that will require an additional 1¼ yd (1.1m) of fabric. To make a half slip, cut the slip fabric to knee length and 1.5 times the waist measurement, then gather and attach to a ½" (1.3cm) wide elastic strip that is 1" (2.6cm) less than the waist measurement.

½" (1.3cm) seams used unless otherwise noted.

Refer to Chapter 1 for basic sewing techniques and information on customizing fit.

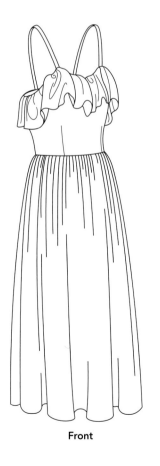

Front

Back

Saltillo Dress

1. Trace off the front and back bodice pieces.

2. Modify the front bodice.

   a. Make a mark on the neckline at about the halfway point of the curve. Draw a line (A) from here to the bust point **(Figure 1)**.

   b. Cut through the center of the waist dart, to but not through the bust point **(Figure 2)**.

   c. Cut the line from the neckline, to but not through the bust point **(Figure 2)**.

   d. Rotate the top half of the bodice so that the neckline overlaps ½" (1.3cm). This will widen the waist dart **(Figure 2)**. Paper under the opened dart.

   e. Make a mark (B) on the center front 4" (10.2cm) down from the neckline edge. Draw a curved

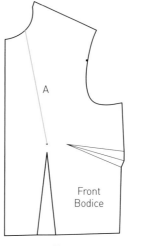

Figure 1

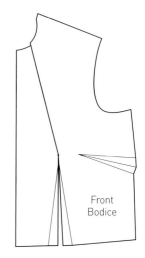

Figure 2

Fabric Needs

Dress Size	If using 44/45" (111.8/114.3cm) fabric, in yards (meters)		If using 58/60" (147.3/152.4cm) fabric, in yards (meters)	
	Bodice (includes lining)	Skirt and Ruffle	Bodice (includes lining)	Skirt and Ruffle
0	1 yd (0.9m)	2¾ yd (2.5m)	1 yd (0.9m)	2¾ yd (2.5m)
2	1 yd (0.9m)	2¾ yd (2.5m)	1 yd (0.9m)	2¾ yd (2.5m)
4	1 yd (0.9m)	2¾ yd (2.5m)	1 yd (0.9m)	2¾ yd (2.5m)
6	1 yd (0.9m)	2¾ yd (2.5m)	1 yd (0.9m)	2¾ yd (2.5m)
8	1 yd (0.9m)	2¾ yd (2.5m)	1 yd (0.9m)	2¾ yd (2.5m)
10	1 yd (0.9m)	2¾ yd (2.5m)	1 yd (0.9m)	2¾ yd (2.5m)
12	1 yd (0.9m)	2¾ yd (2.5m)	1 yd (0.9m)	2¾ yd (2.5m)
14	1¾ yd (1.6m)	3¼ yd (3m)	1 yd (0.9m)	2¾ yd (2.5m)
16	1¾ yd (1.6m)	3¼ yd (3m)	1 yd (0.9m)	2¾ yd (2.5m)
18	1¾ yd (1.6m)	3¼ yd (3m)	1 yd (0.9m)	2¾ yd (2.5m)
20	1¾ yd (1.6m)	3¼ yd (3m)	1 yd (0.9m)	2¾ yd (2.5m)
22	1¾ yd (1.6m)	3¼ yd (3m)	1 yd (0.9m)	2¾ yd (2.5m)

line (C) from this mark to the armhole for the new neckline, curving up to the slashed line on the pattern before curving back down to the armscye (**Figure 3**).

   f. Mark 1" (3.8cm) from the bottom edge of the bodice and draw a horizontal cutline (D).

   g. Cut the bodice along lines C and D (**Figure 4**).

3. Modify the back bodice.

   a. Draw a 90° line (A) from the mark on the armhole of the back bodice to the center back (**Figure 5**).

   b. Extend the center line (B) of the waist dart straight up to touch line A (**Figure 5**).

   c. Redraw the waist dart lines from the bottom of the dart legs to touch the point where line B touches line A (**Figure 5**).

   d. Draw a line (C) from the bottom point of the armhole to the center back that touches the original top of the waist dart (**Figure 5**).

   e. Cut the bodice pattern on line C and the new waist dart legs (**Figure 6**).

   f. Remove the dart piece and tape the remaining back bodice pieces together. Remove 1" (2.6cm) from the bottom edge of the bodice (**Figure 7**).

4. Cut one front bodice piece on the fold and cut two back bodice pieces (mirrored) out of outer fabric. Cut one front bodice piece on the fold and cut two back bodice pieces (mirrored) out of lining fabric. Mark the point where the back bodice pieces are taped together on the top edge; this is where the straps will attach.

5. Measure the neckline of the bodice front and bodice back, then multiply this measurement by 2. Cut the ruffle 5" (12.7cm) tall and this length.

6. Cut two straps 2" (5.1cm) wide by 18" (45.7cm) long.

7. Cut a rectangular skirt to maxi length (see the skirt measurement guide in Chapter 1) and 2 times the waist measurement in width. If you need to cut panels of the skirt to get to the final rectangle size, cut one that is the waist measurement in width and two that are half that, then sew one shorter panel to each side of the longer panel. This way you will have side seams and a center back seam.

8. Sew darts on front bodice and lining (**Figure 8**).

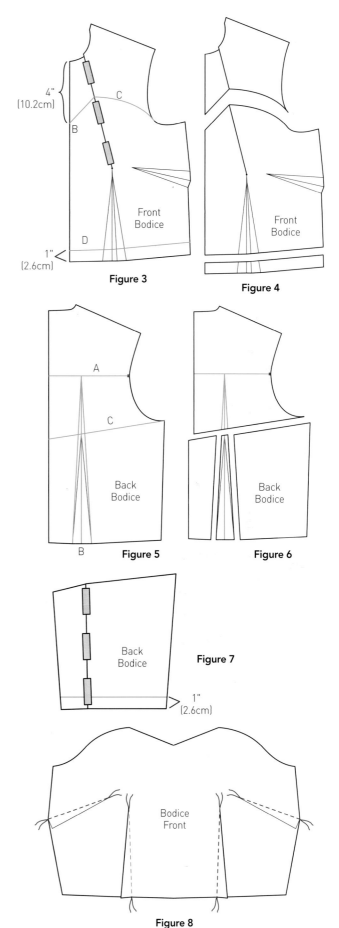

Figure 3

Figure 4

Figure 5

Figure 6

Figure 7

Figure 8

9. Sew the two bodice back pieces to the bodice front along the side seams, right sides together (**Figure 9**). Repeat with lining.

10. Finish one long edge of the ruffle with a narrow hem. Gather the other long edge of the ruffle. Baste the ruffle to the neckline of the bodice, wrong side of the ruffle to the right side of the bodice (**Figure 10**).

11. Finish short raw edges of the skirt with an overlock stitch or faux overlock stitch.

12. Gather the top edge of the skirt to match the width of the bodice at the waistline.

13. Sew the bodice to the skirt along the waistline, right sides together. (**Figure 11**). Press waistline seam toward bodice.

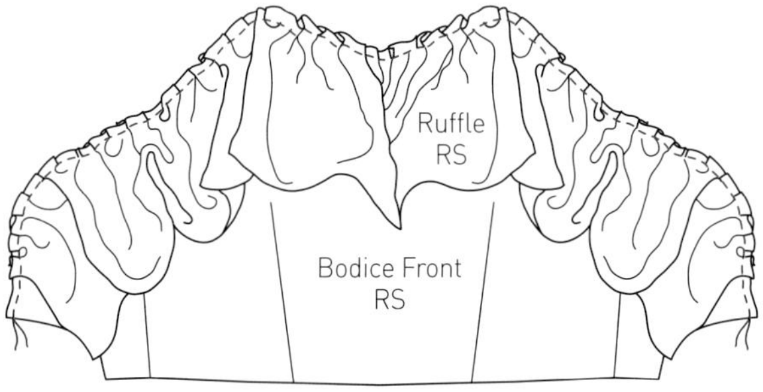

14. Lay the zipper along one side of the center back of the dress and mark the bottom of the zipper.

15. Fold dress right sides together, matching the center back edges. Baste the seam from the top edge to the mark, then backstitch and shorten to a regular stitch length for the rest of the seam. Press seam open.

16. Insert the zipper in the center back seam (**Figure 12**).

17. Press the straps in half, wrong sides together, matching long edges. Open straps. Press raw edges toward the crease line, wrong sides together. Then press again on the original crease line. Your straps should now be ½" (1.3cm) wide. Topstitch down each side of the strap to finish.

18. Pin the straps to the bodice front, directly above each waist dart point, with the straps pointing down. Baste in place (**Figure 13**).

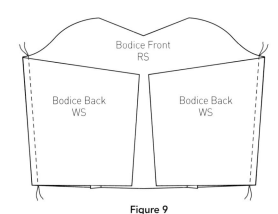

Figure 9

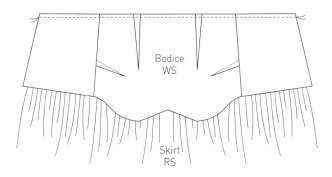

Figure 10

Figure 11

Figure 12
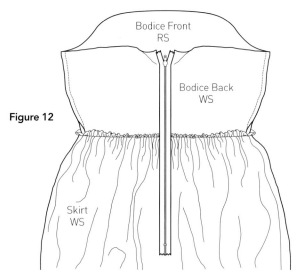

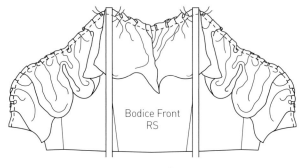

Figure 13

19. Press the bottom edge of the lining ⅜" (1cm) to the wrong side.

20. Pin the bodice lining to the bodice along the neckline edge, right sides together. The lining should extend beyond the zipper ½" (1.3cm) on each side. Stitch the lining to the bodice, leaving ½" (1.3cm) wide openings at the strap marks on the bodice back (**Figure 14**).

21. Clip the corner and points of the front neckline (**Figure 15**).

22. Turn the lining to the inside of the dress. Press the neckline.

23. Turn the center back edges of the lining ½" (1.3cm) to the wrong side and pin, sandwiching the zipper between the lining and the outer fabric. Stitch over the zipper line again, securing the lining.

24. Pin the folded edge of the lining over the waistline seam (**Figure 16**).

25. On the right side of the dress, stitch in the ditch of the waistline seam to secure the lining (**Figure 17**).

26. Push the straps into the openings on the back bodice. Pin. Try the dress on and adjust the straps as needed. Topstitch the neckline edge of the dress, securing the back straps in the process.

27. Turn the bottom edge of the skirt ½" (1.3cm) to the wrong side twice and press to form the hem. Stitch hem.

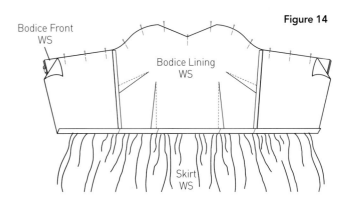

Figure 14

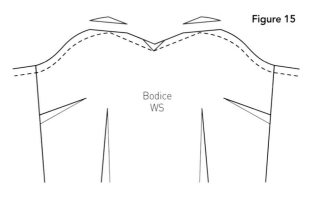

Figure 15

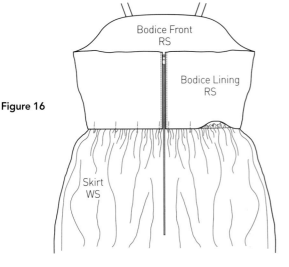

Figure 16

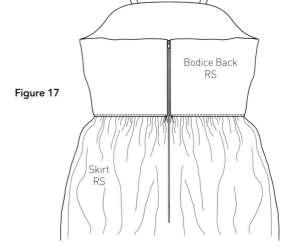

Figure 17

Driskill dress

For any little girl who ever dreamed ballerina dreams, this tulle confection of a dress is sure to inspire a few jetés of joy.

Front

Back

Materials

FABRIC
Shown: Polyester satin (main) and nylon tulle

Dress Size	Main Fabric 44/45" (111.8/ 114.3cm)	or	Main Fabric 58/60" (147.3/ 152.4cm)	Tulle 44/45" (111.8/ 114.3cm)
2T	1⅛ yd (1.1m)		1 yd (0.9m)	8 yd (7.3m)
3T	1⅛ yd (1.1m)		1 yd (0.9m)	8½ yd (7.8m)
4T	1⅛ yd (1.1m)		1 yd (0.9m)	8¾ yd (8m)
5	1⅛ yd (1.1m)		1 yd (0.9m)	9¼ yd (8.5m)
6	1¾ yd (1.6m)	or	1⅛ yd (1.1m)	9¾ yd (8.9m)
8	1¾ yd (1.6m)		1⅛ yd (1.1m)	10 yd (9.1m)
10	1¾ yd (1.6m)		1⅛ yd (1.1m)	10½ yd (9.6m)
12	1¾ yd (1.6m)		1⅛ yd (1.1m)	11⅓ yd (10.4m)

NOTIONS
1 package double-fold bias tape

16" (40.6cm) zipper

NOTES
Main fabric amounts listed include enough for lining in the same fabric. Recalculate if using different material for lining.

½" (1.3cm) seams used unless otherwise noted.

Refer to Chapter 1 for basic sewing techniques and information on customizing fit.

Driskill Dress

1. Trace off the front and back bodice pieces.

2. Modify the front bodice (**Figure 1**).

   a. Redraw the side seam (A) at a 90° angle from the bottom of the armscye (instead of angling in toward the waist).

   b. Draw a horizontal line (B) at the level of the bottom of the armhole.

   c. Measure vertically between the point of the neckline at center front and line B. Draw a horizontal line (C) one-quarter of the distance from the neckline.

   d. Measure the shoulder seam and mark the midpoint. Draw a line at 90° from the midpoint of the shoulder to line C; the point at which this line touches line C is point D.

   e. From point D, draw an angled line (E) merging with the armscye.

   f. Measure vertically between the point of the neckline at center front and line B. Mark a point one-third of the distance from the neckline, then connect this point to point D in a slight curve (F) to form the new neckline.

3. Modify the back bodice by repeating steps 2a–f from the front bodice on the back bodice (**Figure 1**).

4. Cut front and back bodice pattern pieces on lines F, E and A; these will be strapless.

5. Cut the front bodice piece on the fold out of main fabric and out of lining. Cut two back bodice pieces (mirrored) out of main fabric and two (mirrored) out of lining.

6. Measure the new front and back armscye, and add these numbers together. Add 18" (45.7cm) to that number and cut two ½" (1.3cm) wide double-fold bias tape straps this length.

7. For the skirt, cut ten pieces of tulle 3 times the waist measurement in width and knee length (referring to the skirt measurement guide in Chapter 1) plus 2" (5.1cm), and one piece of lining 2 times the waist measurement in width and knee length.

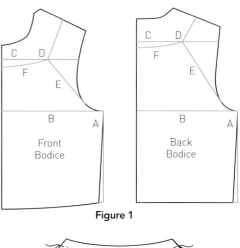

Figure 1

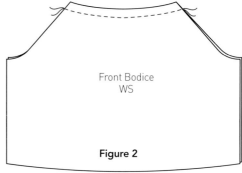

Figure 2

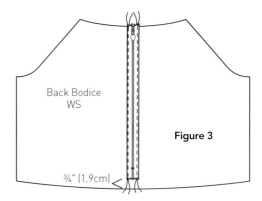

Figure 3

8. Place the bodice front and lining right sides together and sew along the neckline (**Figure 2**). Turn right-side out and press the neckline.

9. Insert a zipper in the center back bodice, making sure the zipper ends ¾" (1.9cm) above the waist-line edge (**Figure 3**). To shorten the zipper, stitch across the zipper teeth using a wide zigzag stitch set to the shortest stitch length possible.

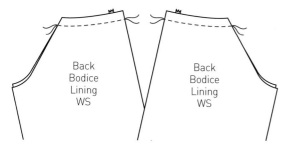

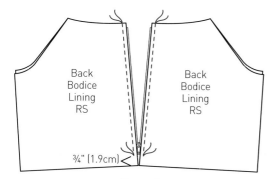

Figure 4

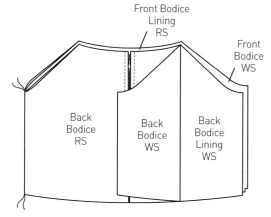

¾" (1.9cm)

Figure 5

Front Bodice
Lining
RS

Front
Bodice
WS

Back
Bodice
RS

Back
Bodice
WS

Back
Bodice
Lining
WS

Figure 6

Front Bodice
WS

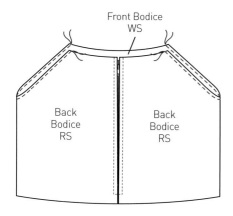

Back
Bodice
RS

Back
Bodice
RS

Figure 7

10. Unzip the back bodice and place the back lining and back bodice pieces right sides together. The lining will extend ½" (1.3cm) past the zipper. Stitch the neckline edges (**Figure 4**).

11. Turn the back bodice right-side out and press the neckline. Press the lining edge to the wrong side and pin along the zipper tape. Stitch in the same line that attached the zipper. Leave the last ¾" (1.9cm) of the lining above the waistline unsewn (**Figure 5**).

12. Match the front and back bodice right sides together along the side seams, and the front and back lining right sides together at the side seams. Sew all four side seams, then turn the bodice right-side out (**Figure 6**). *Note:* Figure 6 shows the right side unsewn, so the order of layers can be seen.

13. Baste the armscyes (**Figure 7**).

14. Fold the bodice to work with one armscye. Take one of the straps and match the strap center with the side seam. Unfold the bias tape and pin along the armscye. Stitch in the crease closest to the raw edge (**Figure 8**).

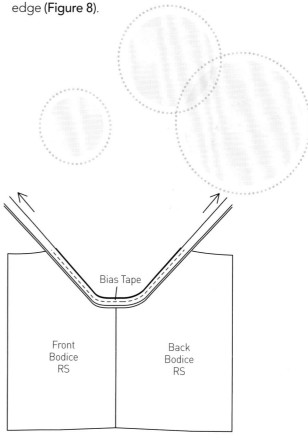

Bias Tape

Front
Bodice
RS

Back
Bodice
RS

Figure 8

15. Fold the bias tape to the wrong side, making sure to cover the seam from step 14. Stitch on the right side, close to the seam, making sure to catch the bias tape on the wrong side. Continue to stitch the edges of the bias tape together to form the straps, folding the short ends of the bias tape to the inside and sewing across the ends to enclose all raw edges (**Figure 9**).

16. Layer the tulle, matching top edges as best as possible. Use clips to hold the layers together (I use Wonder clips). Stitch the layers together across the top edge, then trim the tulle along the top and bottom edges so that it is straight (this is what the 2" [2.6cm] beyond knee length is for).

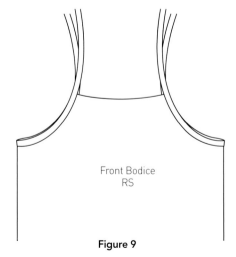

Front Bodice
RS

Figure 9

17. Fold the skirt lining right sides together, matching the short edges. Stitch the short edges; finish this seam. Turn one raw edge ½" (1.3cm) to the wrong side twice, forming a hem. Stitch the hem.

18. Gather the tulle width along the top edge to the almost the same width as the skirt. Leave the tulle long enough that the sides can overlap 1" (2.6cm) at the center back. Place the tulle wrong side against the skirt right side, overlapping 1" (2.6cm) at center back; this helps you avoid visible seams in the tulle. Stitch in place over the gathering stitches. The tulle should hang about ½" (1.3cm) to 1" (2.6cm) lower than the bottom of the skirt lining. Remove the gathering threads.

19. Gather the tulle plus skirt lining combination (skirt) to the same width as the bodice (**Figure 10**).

20. Turn the skirt right-side out. The skirt seam is the center back. Fold the skirt to mark the center front. Gather the top edge of the skirt to match the width of the bodice at the waistline.

21. Press the bottom edge of the bodice lining ⅜" (1cm) to the wrong side.

22. Turn the bodice wrong-side out.

23. Put the skirt inside the bodice, matching bodice (not lining) and skirt waistlines, center back and center front. Stitch this seam (**Figure 11**).

24. Pin the folded edge of the lining over the waistline seam. On the right side of the dress, stitch in the ditch of the waistline seam to secure the lining, or secure with a slipstitch.

Bodice

Skirt

Figure 10

Bodice
WS

Bodice
Lining
WS

Skirt
RS

Figure 11

This dress is adorable in the winter under a Nordic sweater with tights and warm boots.

Mayfield dress

The bodice of this sundress gets textural detail from over-the-bust gathers to add interest to a classic silhouette. Wear on a date or gallivanting around town for effortless summer style.

Front

Back

Materials

FABRIC
Shown: Embroidered cotton voile

Dress Size	44/45" (111.8/114.3cm)	or	58/60" (147.3/152.4cm)
0	2¾ yd (2.5m)		1⅓ yd (1.2m)
2	2¾ yd (2.5m)		1⅓ yd (1.2m)
4	2¾ yd (2.5m)		1⅓ yd (1.2m)
6	2¾ yd (2.5m)		1⅓ yd (1.2m)
8	2¾ yd (2.5m)		1⅓ yd (1.2m)
10	2¾ yd (2.5m)		2¾ yd (2.5m)
12	2¾ yd (2.5m)	or	2¾ yd (2.5m)
14	3¼ yd (3m)		2¾ yd (2.5m)
16	3¼ yd (3m)		2¾ yd (2.5m)
18	3¼ yd (3m)		2¾ yd (2.5m)
20	3¼ yd (3m)		2¾ yd (2.5m)
22	3¼ yd (3m)		2¾ yd (2.5m)

NOTIONS
14" (35.6cm) zipper

Interfacing that matches the weight of the fabric, for bodice (optional)

NOTES
Fabric amounts listed include enough for lining in the same fabric. Recalculate if using different material for lining.

½" (1.3cm) seams used unless otherwise noted.

Refer to Chapter 1 for basic sewing techniques and information on customizing fit.

Mayfield Dress

1. Trace off the front and back bodice pieces.

2. Modify the front bodice.

   a. Make a mark on the neckline at about the halfway point of the curve. Draw a line (A) from here to the bust point (**Figure 1**).

   b. Cut through the center of the waist dart, to but not through the bust point (**Figure 2**).

   c. Cut the line from the neckline, to but not through the bust point (**Figure 2**).

   d. Rotate the top half of the bodice so that the neckline overlaps ½" (1.3cm). This will widen the waist dart (**Figure 2**).

   e. Make a mark (B) on the center front 2¾" (7cm) down from the neckline edge. Draw a curved line (C) from this mark to the armhole for the new neckline (**Figure 3**).

   f. Cut the bodice along line C (**Figure 3**). This will be the bodice lining. Trace off this piece again to create the front bodice pieces.

   g. Using the new tracing, mark off the top and bottom 2" (5.1cm) of the bodice and cut along these lines (**Figure 4**).

   h. On the bottom section of the bodice, cut out and remove the dart area and tape the remaining two pieces back together (**Figure 5**).

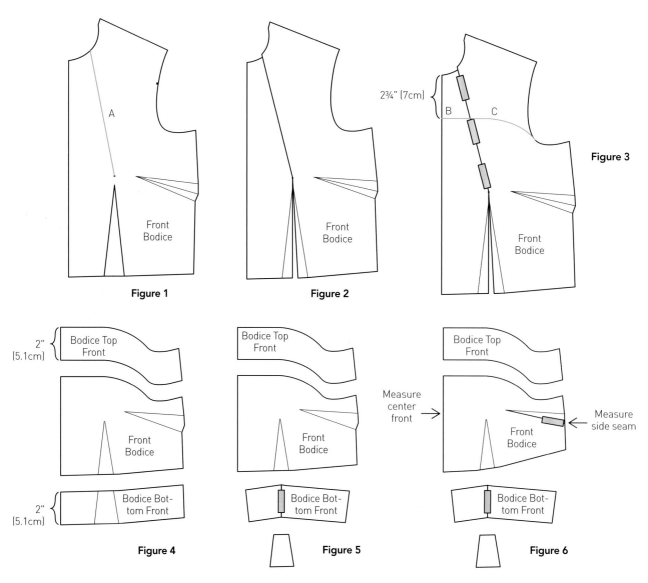

Figure 1 Figure 2 Figure 3

Figure 4 Figure 5 Figure 6

i. Fold the side dart closed on the center bodice piece; pin or tape closed. Measure this portion of the bodice at the center front and at the side seam (**Figure 6**). Add 2" (5.1cm) to each of these measurements.

(1) Center front measurement:

_____ + 2" (5.1cm) = _____

(2) Side seam measurement:

_____ + 2" (5.1cm) = _____

j. Fold and tape or pin the waist dart closed on the center portion of the bodice. Measure the width of the bodice portion at the waist (**Figure 7**). Multiply this number by 1.5.

(3) Lower front measurement:

_____ × 1.5 = _____

k. Create a new center bodice portion. Draw a vertical line (A) the same length as the recorded center front measurement for the center front. At the center of this line, draw a horizontal line (B) the length of the recorded lower front measurement. At the end of the horizontal line, draw a vertical line (C) the length of the recorded side seam measurement. This vertical line should be centered on the horizontal line. Join the ends of each vertical line to create a trapezoid shape (**Figure 8**). This is the front bust piece.

l. Add 2" (2.6cm) to the recorded center front measurement. Make a rectangular pattern piece this length and 3" (7.6cm) wide. This will be the center front bodice piece (**Figure 8**).

3. Modify the back bodice.

a. Draw a 90° line (A) from the mark on the armhole of the back bodice to the center back (**Figure 9**).

b. Extend the center line (B) of the waist dart straight up to touch line A (**Figure 9**).

c. Redraw the waist dart lines from the bottom of the dart legs to touch the point where line B touches line A (**Figure 9**).

d. Draw a line (C) from the bottom point of the armhole to the center back that touches the original top of the waist dart (**Figure 9**).

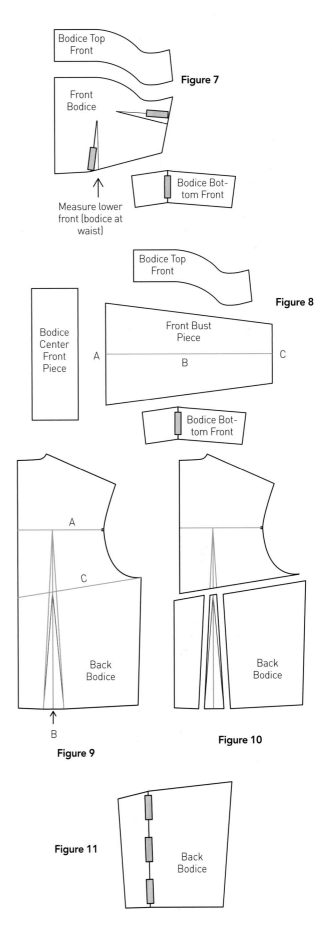

Figure 7

Measure lower front (bodice at waist)

Figure 8

Figure 9

Figure 10

Figure 11

e. Cut the bodice pattern on line C and the new waist dart legs (**Figure 10**).

f. Remove the dart piece and tape the remaining back bodice pieces together (**Figure 11**).

4. Cut one of the bodice front linings on the fold. Cut one center front bodice piece out of main fabric. Cut two front bust pieces, two top front bodice pieces and two bottom front bodice pieces out of main fabric; mirror all pieces. If desired, cut two top front bodice pieces and two bottom front bodice pieces out of interfacing as well. Cut two back bodice pieces (mirrored) out of outer fabric and two out of lining. Mark the point where the back bodice pieces are taped together on the top edge; this is where the straps will attach.

5. Cut two straps 2" (5.1cm) wide by 18" (45.7cm) long.

6. Cut a rectangular skirt to knee length (see the skirt measurement guide in Chapter 1) and 2 times the waist measurement in width. If you need to cut panels of the skirt to get to the final rectangle size, cut one that is the waist measurement in width and two that are half that, then sew one shorter panel to each side of the longer panel. This way you will have side seams and a center back seam.

7. Sew the darts on the front bodice lining (**Figure 12**).

8. Sew gathering stitches along the top and bottom of each front bust piece. Gather the top edge of each piece the same width as the top front bodice piece, and gather the bottom to the same width as the bottom front bodice piece (**Figure 13**).

9. Sew the top bodice pieces to the bust front pieces right sides together. Sew the bottom bodice pieces to the bust front pieces right sides together (**Figure 14**).

10. Pin the center front bodice piece right sides together with one side of the front bodice and stitch. Pin right sides together with the other side of the bodice and stitch (**Figure 15**).

11. Sew the two bodice back pieces to the bodice front along the side seams, right sides together (**Figure 16**). Repeat with lining.

12. Finish the short raw edges of the skirt with an overlock stitch or faux overlock stitch.

13. Gather the top edge of the skirt to match the width of the bodice at the waistline.

14. Sew the bodice to the skirt along the waistline, right sides together (**Figure 17**). Press waistline seam toward bodice.

15. Lay the zipper along one side of the center back of the dress and mark the bottom of the zipper.

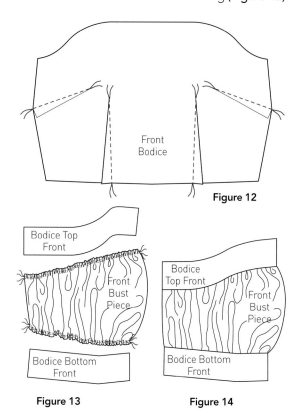

Front Bodice

Figure 12

Bodice Top Front

Front Bust Piece

Bodice Bottom Front

Figure 13

Bodice Top Front

Front Bust Piece

Bodice Bottom Front

Figure 14

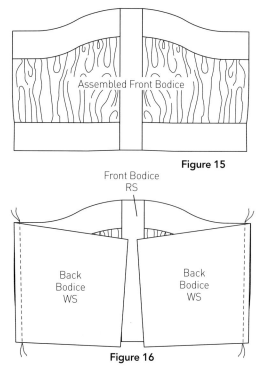

Assembled Front Bodice

Figure 15

Front Bodice RS

Back Bodice WS

Back Bodice WS

Figure 16

16. Fold the dress right sides together, matching the center back edges. Baste the seam from the top edge to the mark, then backstitch and shorten to a regular stitch length for the rest of the seam. Press seam open.

17. Insert the zipper in the center back seam (**Figure 18**).

18. Press the straps in half, wrong sides together, matching long edges. Open straps. Press raw edges toward the crease line, wrong sides together. Then press again on the original crease line. Your straps should now be ½" (1.3cm) wide. Topstitch down each side of the strap to finish.

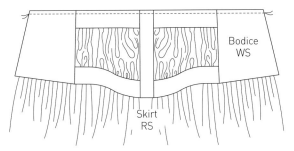

Figure 17

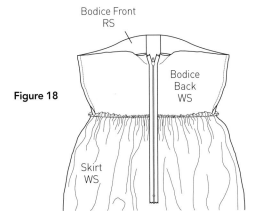

Figure 18

19. Pin the straps to the bodice front, directly above each waist dart point, with the straps pointing down. Baste in place.

20. Press the bottom edge of the lining ⅜" (1cm) to the wrong side.

21. Pin the bodice lining to the bodice along the neckline edge, right sides together (**Figure 19**). The lining should extend beyond the zipper ½" (1.3cm) on each side. Stitch the lining to the bodice, leaving ½" (1.3cm) wide openings at the strap marks on the bodice back.

22. Turn the lining to the inside of the dress. Press the neckline.

23. Turn the center back edges of the lining ½" (1.3cm) to the wrong side and pin, sandwiching the zipper between the lining and the outer fabric. Stitch over the zipper line again, securing the lining.

24. Pin the folded edge of the lining over the waistline seam (**Figure 20**).

25. On the right side of the dress, stitch in the ditch of the waistline seam to secure the lining (**Figure 21**).

26. Push the straps into the openings on the back bodice. Pin. Try dress on and adjust straps as needed. Topstitch neckline edge of dress, securing the back straps in the process.

27. Turn the bottom edge of the skirt ½" (1.3cm) to the wrong side twice and press to form the hem. Stitch hem.

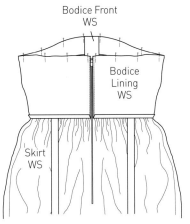

Figure 19

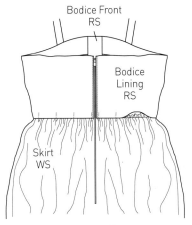

Figure 20

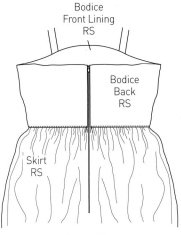

Figure 21

Oasis dress

The Oasis Dress has couture details that are perfect for an event like a summer wedding. The fully lined dress features an asymmetrical neckline, bubble skirt and front gathering that make it truly special.

Front

Back

Materials

FABRIC
Shown: 50-50 silk/cotton blend

Dress Size	44/45" (111.8/114.3cm)	or	58/60" (147.3/152.4cm)
2T	2 yd (1.8m)		2 yd (1.8m)
3T	2 yd (1.8m)		2 yd (1.8m)
4T	2 yd (1.8m)		2 yd (1.8m)
5	2 yd (1.8m)		2 yd (1.8m)
6	2⅓ yd (2.1m)	or	2⅓ yd (2.1m)
8	2⅓ yd (2.1m)		2⅓ yd (2.1m)
10	2⅓ yd (2.1m)		2⅓ yd (2.1m)
12	2⅓ yd (2.1m)		2⅓ yd (2.1m)

NOTIONS
12" (30.5cm) zipper

NOTES
Fabric amounts listed include enough for lining in the same fabric. Recalculate if using different material for lining.

½" (1.3cm) seams used unless otherwise noted.

Refer to Chapter 1 for basic sewing techniques and information on customizing fit.

Oasis Dress

1. Trace off the front bodice piece, then flip it over, lining it up to the center front line and tracing again, so that you have a full bodice to start with. Trace off the back bodice, repeating this process and making sure to remove the amount added along the center back for the zipper.

2. Modify the front bodice.

   a. Draw a diagonal line (A) from the armscye to the right shoulder, barely touching the neckline. Cut pattern on this line **(Figure 1)**.

   b. Cut pattern on the center front line from the neckline to, but not through, the waistline. Rotate the pieces so that they overlap ½" (1.3cm) on the neckline edge. Add paper under the pattern and redraw the neckline. This is your front lining piece **(Figure 2)**.

   c. Trace a copy of the front lining piece to create the bodice front.

   d. Draw three evenly spaced diagonal lines from the shoulder to the waistline. Cut pattern along these lines. The lines should be evenly spaced from the center of the shoulder and at least ¾" (1.9cm) away from the pattern edges, then radiate to the waist center. It's easiest to draw the first line (B) from center shoulder to center waist then space the other two lines **(Figure 3)**.

   e. Spread the four pattern pieces so there is a 1" (2.6cm) gap between each piece. Paper over the gaps to create your front bodice piece **(Figure 4)**.

3. Modify the back bodice by repeating steps 2a–b from the front bodice on the back bodice.

4. Cut front and back bodice pattern pieces out of main fabric. *Note:* Be VERY careful—cut with the fabric RIGHT-side up, the front bodice RIGHT-side up, and the back bodice WRONG-side up. The front and back bodices should be mirror images.

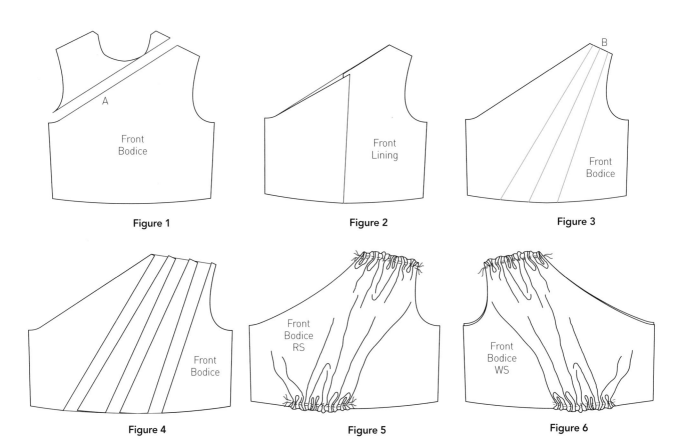

Figure 1

Figure 2

Figure 3

Figure 4

Figure 5

Figure 6

5. Cut the front lining and back bodice pieces out of lining. *Note:* Be VERY careful—cut with the fabric RIGHT-side up, the front bodice WRONG-side up, and the back bodice RIGHT-side up. The front lining piece should be a mirror image of the front bodice, and the back lining piece should be a mirror image of the back bodice.

6. On the front bodice, mark the outermost cuts (outermost lines from step 2d) you made on the pattern on both the shoulder and neckline edges. These are your gathering marks.

7. Cut two skirt pieces to midi length (see the skirt measurement guide in Chapter 1) and 1.5 times the waist measurement in width.

8. Cut the skirt lining to knee length and 1.5 times the waist measurement.

9. Gather the front bodice in between the marks on the shoulder and waistline, so that the front bodice matches the front lining piece (**Figure 5**). Sew another line of stitching over the gathers to secure.

10. Pin the front bodice to the back bodice at the shoulder, right sides together, and stitch (**Figure 6**). Repeat this step with the front and back lining.

11. Pin the outer bodice to the lining, right sides together, along the neckline and armhole edges, matching the shoulder seams. Stitch neckline and armhole edges (**Figure 7**). Clip curves.

12. Place the outer front bodice right sides together with the outer back bodice. Match the side seam edges together on the non-shoulder side. Baste the non-shoulder side of the outer bodice pieces together (**Figure 8**); this is the side the zipper will be inserted on.

13. Place the skirt pieces right sides together, matching the side edges. Stitch one side seam.

14. Gather the top edge to match the width of the bodice at the waistline (**Figure 9**).

15. Stitch the outer bodice to the skirt at the waistline, right sides together, matching the side seams. Press the waist seam toward the bodice. Insert a zipper into the side seam.

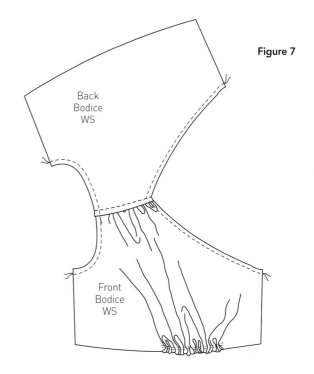

Figure 7

Back Bodice WS

Front Bodice WS

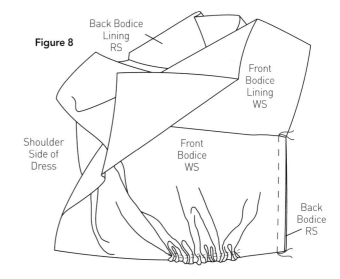

Figure 8

Back Bodice Lining RS

Front Bodice Lining WS

Shoulder Side of Dress

Front Bodice WS

Back Bodice RS

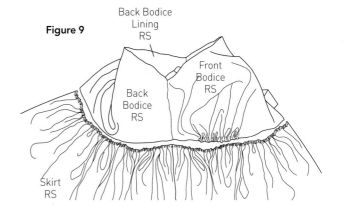

Figure 9

Back Bodice Lining RS

Front Bodice RS

Back Bodice RS

Skirt RS

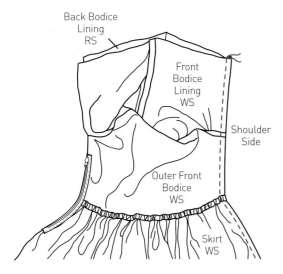

Back Bodice Lining RS

Front Bodice Lining WS

Shoulder Side

Outer Front Bodice WS

Skirt WS

Figure 10

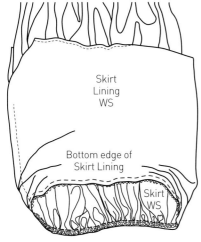

Skirt Lining WS

Bottom edge of Skirt Lining

Skirt WS

Figure 11

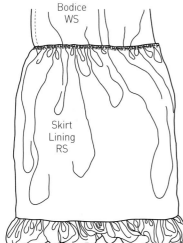

Bodice WS

Skirt Lining RS

Figure 12

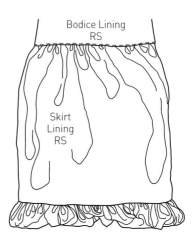

Bodice Lining RS

Skirt Lining RS

Figure 13

16. Fold the dress right sides together and match the outer front bodice to the back bodice on the shoulder side. Match the front lining to the back lining at the side seam, and match the skirt side seam. Stitch this side seam in one long seam (**Figure 10**).

17. Place the skirt lining piece right sides together, matching the side edges. Measure how much of the zipper extends below the waistline of the skirt. Measure this amount down from the top of the skirt lining and make a mark. Stitch the side seam of the skirt lining from the mark to the bottom.

18. Sew gathering stitches around the top edge of the skirt lining.

19. Gather the bottom edge of the skirt to match the width of the skirt lining.

20. Place the skirt inside the skirt lining, right sides together, matching the bottom edges. Stitch the bottom edge of the skirt to the lining (**Figure 11**).

21. Flip the skirt lining to the inside of the dress, so that the lining is wrong sides together with the skirt. Gather the top of the skirt lining to match the waistline of the skirt, then stitch the lining to the seam allowance of the dress waistline (**Figure 12**). The top of the skirt lining side seam that was left open should be turned under and hand-stitched to the zipper tape.

22. Fold the bodice lining raw edges ⅜" (1cm) to the wrong side and press. Pin the lining open side seams to barely cover the zipper stitching on the wrong side of the bodice. Hand-stitch the lining to the zipper tape.

23. Pin the pressed waist edge of the lining to cover the waist seam. Hand-stitch the bodice lining to the skirt lining (**Figure 13**).

Rosedale dress

A charming maxi from the front, this dress is a showstopper in the back with crossed straps topped with a bow. Echoing the vintage charm of the neighborhood it's named after, the Rosedale Dress captures the sweet nostalgia of summer.

Front

Back

Materials

FABRIC
Shown: Cotton voile

Dress Size	44/45" (111.8/114.3cm)	or	58/60" (147.3/152.4cm)
2T	2½ yd (2.3m)		2½ yd (2.3m)
3T	2½ yd (2.3m)		2½ yd (2.3m)
4T	2¾ yd (2.5m)		2¾ yd (2.5m)
5	2¾ yd (2.5m)		2¾ yd (2.5m)
6	3¾ yd (3.4m)	or	2¾ yd (2.5m)
8	3¾ yd (3.4m)		2⅞ yd (2.6m)
10	3¾ yd (3.4m)		2⅞ yd (2.6m)
12	3¾ yd (3.4m)		2⅞ yd (2.6m)

NOTIONS
½ yd (0.5m) of ¾" (1.9cm) wide elastic

Interfacing that matches the weight of the fabric, for bodice (optional)

NOTES
Fabric amounts listed include enough for lining in the same fabric. Recalculate if using different material for lining.

½" (1.3cm) seams used unless otherwise noted.

Refer to Chapter 1 for basic sewing techniques and information on customizing fit.

Rosedale Dress

1. Trace off the front bodice piece.

2. Modify the front bodice.

   a. Draw a horizontal line (A) at the level of the bottom of the armhole (**Figure 1**).

   b. Measure vertically between the neckline and line A. Mark a point (B) one-quarter of the way down from the neckline (**Figure 1**).

   c. Measure the side seam. Mark a point (C) one-quarter of the way down from line A. Draw a curved line to connect the two points (**Figure 1**).

   d. Draw a new waistline 1" (2.6cm) higher than the waistline and cut the front pattern piece as shown (**Figure 2**).

3. Draw the back bodice, which will be created.

   a. Start with a rectangle that is one-half the waist measurement long and 2" (5.1cm) high.

   b. Curve the last 3" (7.6cm) of the rectangle up to the same side seam length as the front bodice (**Figure 3**).

   c. Add a ½" (1.3cm) seam allowance to the side of the back bodice piece (**Figure 4**).

4. Cut the front bodice piece on the fold out of main fabric and out of lining. Cut two back bodice pieces out of main fabric and out of lining. If desired, cut interfacing for the front and back bodice pieces to add stability to the bodice.

5. Cut skirt to maxi length (see the skirt measurement guide in Chapter 1) and 2 times the waist measurement in width. If needed, cut two panels to get the needed width.

6. Cut two straps that are 3" (7.6cm) wide and the appropriate length from the chart below:

Dress Size	Strap Length
2T	16" (40.6cm)
3T	16½" (41.9cm)
4T	17" (43.2cm)
5	17½" (44.5cm)
6	18" (45.7cm)
8	19" (48.3cm)
10	20" (50.8cm)
12	21" (53.3cm)

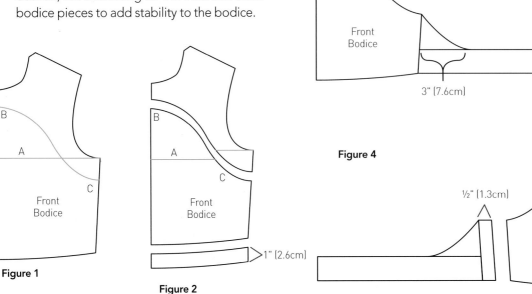

Figure 3

Front Bodice

2" (5.1cm)

3" (7.6cm)

Figure 4

½" (1.3cm)

Front Bodice

Figure 1

Front Bodice

Figure 2

Front Bodice

1" (2.6cm)

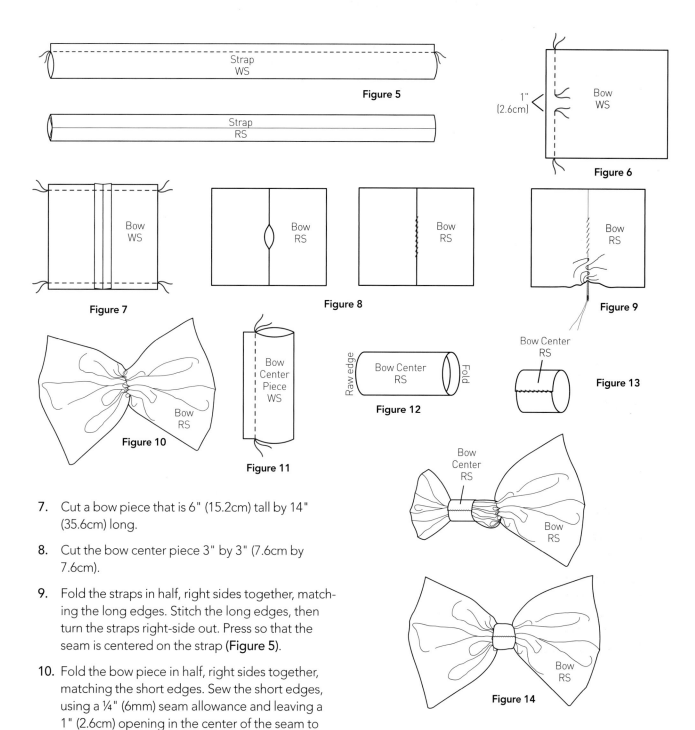

Figure 5

Figure 6

Figure 7

Figure 8

Figure 9

Figure 10

Figure 11

Figure 12

Figure 13

Figure 14

7. Cut a bow piece that is 6" (15.2cm) tall by 14" (35.6cm) long.

8. Cut the bow center piece 3" by 3" (7.6cm by 7.6cm).

9. Fold the straps in half, right sides together, matching the long edges. Stitch the long edges, then turn the straps right-side out. Press so that the seam is centered on the strap (**Figure 5**).

10. Fold the bow piece in half, right sides together, matching the short edges. Sew the short edges, using a ¼" (6mm) seam allowance and leaving a 1" (2.6cm) opening in the center of the seam to turn the bow later (**Figure 6**).

11. Refold the bow to center the seam. Stitch across the open ends, using a ¼" (6mm) seam allowance (**Figure 7**). Clip the corners.

12. Turn the bow right side out and press. Hand-stitch the bow opening closed (**Figure 8**).

13. Hand-stitch a basting seam through the center of the bow, through both layers (**Figure 9**).

14. Gather the bow in the center (**Figure 10**).

15. Fold the bow center piece in half, right sides together. Stitch, using a ¼" (6mm) seam allowance (**Figure 11**). Turn the tube right-side out.

16. Push one end of the bow ¼" (6mm) toward the inside (**Figure 12**).

17. Push the raw edge of the bow center into the folded edge, forming a loop. Hand-stitch the loop closed (**Figure 13**).

18. Push the bow through the bow center (**Figure 14**).

19. Sew the back bodice pieces to the bodice front at the side seams (**Figure 15**). Repeat with lining.

20. Pin the straps, seam-side up, to the front bodice. Baste in place (**Figure 16**).

21. Fold the bodice right sides together and sew the center back seam (**Figure 17**). Repeat with lining.

22. Place the lining and bodice right sides together. Stitch together along upper edge, securing straps in between bodice and lining. Leave openings for straps on the back bodice pieces approximately 1" (2.6cm) in from each side seam (**Figure 18**).

23. Fold the skirt right sides together, matching short edges. Stitch. Finish this seam.

24. The skirt seam is the center back. Fold skirt to mark the center front, then refold, matching center front and center back. Mark the sides while the skirt is folded like this. In other words, mark the skirt in quarters.

25. Gather the front half of the skirt to the same width as the front bodice (**Figure 19**).

26. Gather the back half of the skirt to the same width as the back bodice.

27. Press the raw edge of the bodice lining ⅜" (1cm) to the wrong side.

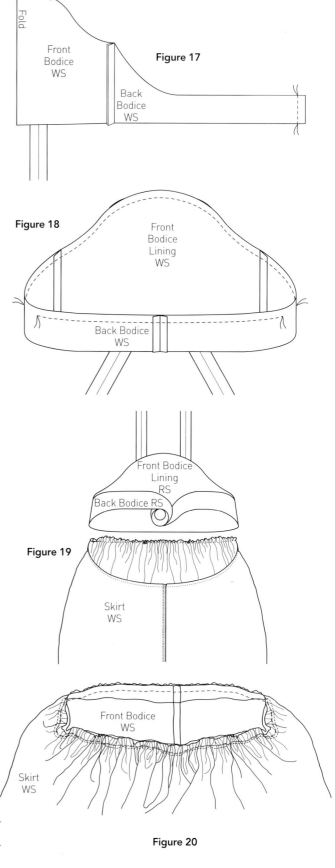

Figure 17

Figure 18

Figure 19

Figure 20

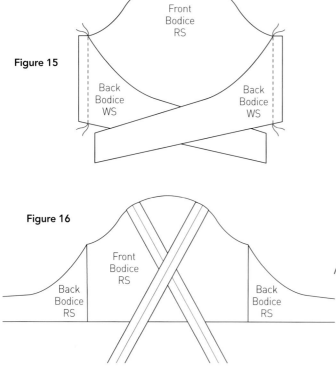

Figure 15

Figure 16

28. With the skirt wrong-side out and the bodice right-side out, place the bodice inside the skirt, matching the bodice front with the skirt front, and the bodice back with the skirt back. Adjust gathers as needed and stitch (**Figure 20**).

29. On the wrong side of the dress, pin the folded edge of the lining over the waist seam. On the right side of the fabric, stitch in the ditch to secure the lining, or secure with a slipstitch. Leave an opening to insert elastic near each side seam (**Figure 21**).

30. Cut a piece of ¾" (1.9cm) wide elastic to one-half of the waist measurement. Using a safety pin, insert the elastic through the back bodice channel, stitching the ends of the elastic into the side seams (**Figure 22**). Stitch the elastic openings closed (**Figure 23**).

31. Cross the straps and insert into the back bodice. Adjust the length as needed and topstitch in place, closing the strap openings (**Figure 24**).

32. Hand-stitch the bow over the crossed straps in the back.

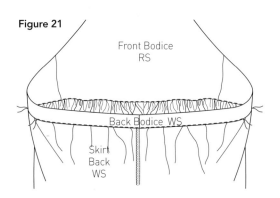

Figure 21

Front Bodice
RS

Back Bodice WS

Skirt Back WS

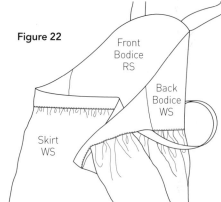

Figure 22

Front Bodice RS

Back Bodice WS

Skirt WS

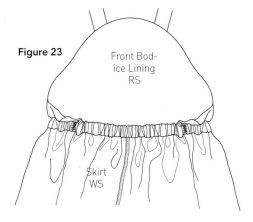

Figure 23

Front Bodice Lining RS

Skirt WS

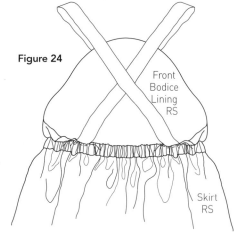

Figure 24

Front Bodice Lining RS

Skirt RS

Lady Bird dress

Lace trim and a cut-away overskirt add special-occasion elegance to this sundress. Girly girls will adore the princess-worthy details, whether it's worn to a wedding or high tea in the playroom.

Front

Back

Materials

FABRIC
Shown: 50-50 silk/cotton blend

Dress Size	44/45" (111.8/114.3cm)	or	58/60" (147.3/152.4cm)
2T	2⅔ yd (2.4m)		2⅔ yd (2.4m)
3T	2⅔ yd (2.4m)		2⅔ yd (2.4m)
4T	2⅔ yd (2.4m)		2⅔ yd (2.4m)
5	2⅔ yd (2.4m)		2⅔ yd (2.4m)
6	4⅓ yd (4m)	or	2⅔ yd (2.4m)
8	4⅓ yd (4m)		2⅔ yd (2.4m)
10	4⅓ yd (4m)		2⅔ yd (2.4m)
12	4⅓ yd (4m)		2⅔ yd (2.4m)

NOTIONS
½ yd (0.5m) of 1" (2.6cm) wide elastic

4 yd (3.7m) of 1"–2" (2.6cm–5.1cm) wide lace

2 yd (1.8m) of 3"–5" (7.6cm–12.7cm) wide lace, finished on both edges and gathered*

1½"–2" (3.8cm–5.1cm) decorative button

NOTES
Fabric amounts listed include enough for lining in the same fabric. Recalculate if using different material for lining.

½" (1.3cm) seams used unless otherwise noted.

Refer to Chapter 1 for basic sewing techniques and information on customizing fit.

*Choose the lace based on the look you want. Gathered lace with both edges finished is shown.

Lady Bird Dress

1. Trace off the front and back bodice pieces.

2. Modify the front bodice (**Figures 1 and 2**).

   a. Redraw the side seam (A) at a 90° angle from the bottom of the armscye (instead of angling in toward the waist).

   b. Draw a horizontal line (B) at the level of the bottom of the armhole.

   c. Draw the seam allowance (C) on the shoulder seam.

   d. Determine the center of the shoulder on line C and make a mark (D). Measure vertically from that point to line B and mark the midway point. Draw a horizontal line (E) at this point to the center front bodice for the new neckline.

   e. At the midpoint mark (D) of the shoulder seam, measure 1¼" (3.2cm) to either side of this mark for the straps. Connect diagonal strap lines (F) to the neckline (E). The straps should remain 2½" (6.4cm) wide—1¼" (3.2cm) to each side of the center.

   f. Find the outer point where the strap meets the neckline. Draw a diagonal line (G) from this point sloping down toward the armhole.

   g. Draw a horizontal line (H) 2" (5.1cm) above the waistline.

3. Modify the back bodice by repeating steps 2a–g from the front bodice on the back bodice (**Figure 3**).

4. Cut the front and back bodice pattern pieces, saving the strap pieces including the shoulder seam allowances (**Figures 4 and 5**).

5. Cut the front and back bodice pieces on the fold out of main fabric and out of lining.

6. Cut a skirt panel to 2 times the waist measurement in width and midi length (see the skirt measurement guide in Chapter 1), minus the width of your wider lace. Cut an overskirt panel to the same width but 1" (2.6cm) shorter.

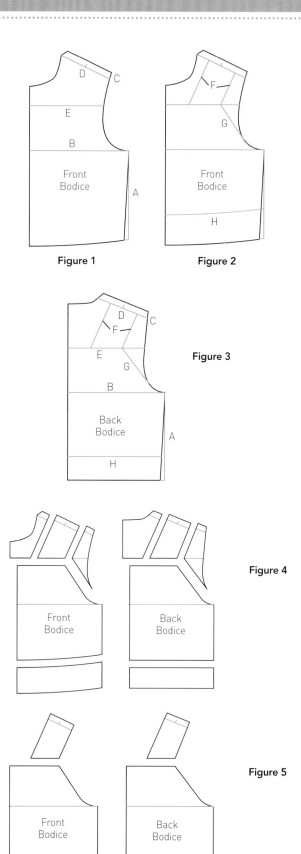

Figure 1

Figure 2

Figure 3

Figure 4

Figure 5

7. Cut a rectangle to the specified size from the chart shown for the shoulder wrap:

Dress Size	Height × Length
2T	8" × 33" (20.3cm × 83.8cm)
3T	8" × 34" (20.3cm × 86.4cm)
4T	8" × 35" (20.3cm × 88.9cm)
5	8" × 36" (20.3cm × 91.4cm)
6	8" × 37" (20.3cm × 94cm)
8	8" × 38½" (20.3cm × 97.8cm)
10	8" × 40" (20.3cm × 101.6cm)
12	8" × 41½" (20.3cm × 105.4cm)

8. Tape the shoulder edges of the strap pieces together, forming a trapezoid (**Figure 6**). This is your elastic length guide for the straps. Cut two ½" (1.3cm) wide pieces of elastic to this length.

9. Untape the center of the strap piece. Spread the two pieces 3" (7.6cm) apart to form a longer trapezoid (**Figure 7**). This is the strap pattern piece; cut two straps from fabric, with the longest edge placed on a fold.

10. Fold the straps right sides together, matching the longest edges, and stitch, using a ¼" (6mm) seam allowance. Turn the strap tubes right-side out. Thread elastic through each strap, scrunching the strap onto the elastic. Baste the ends of the straps to the elastic (**Figure 8**).

11. Pin the straps to the front bodice, ¾" (1.9cm) in from each armhole edge (**Figure 9**).

12. Pin the front bodice lining to the front bodice and stitch the neckline and armhole edges (**Figure 10**). Clip corners, turn right-side out and press.

13. Pin the straps to the back bodice ¾" (1.9cm) in from each armhole edge (**Figure 11**). Pin the back bodice lining over the back bodice and stitch the neckline and armhole edges.

14. Clip the back bodice corners, turn right-side out and press.

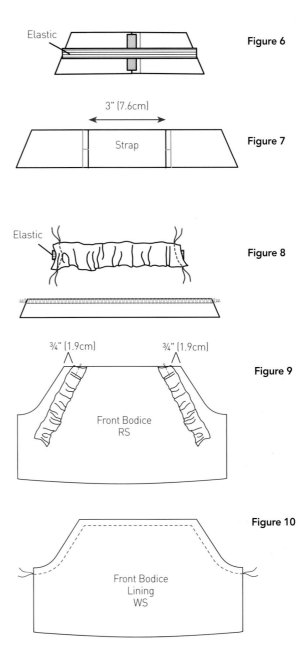

Figure 6

3" (7.6cm)
Strap

Figure 7

Elastic

Figure 8

¾" (1.9cm)   ¾" (1.9cm)

Front Bodice RS

Figure 9

Front Bodice Lining WS

Figure 10

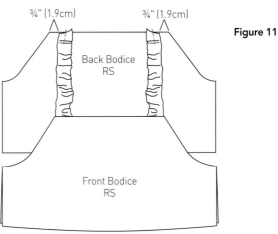

¾" (1.9cm)   ¾" (1.9cm)

Back Bodice RS

Figure 11

Front Bodice RS

15. Place the back bodice and front bodice with lining sides together. Fold the outer sides up, so that the outer fabric is right sides together, and match the side seam edges and armhole seams. Match the side seam edges and armhole seams of the lining to each other as well. Stitch the lining and outer fabric in one seam for each side (**Figures 12–14**).

16. Fold the shoulder rectangle right sides together, matching the long edges. Stitch into a tube, leaving a 3" (7.6cm) gap in the seam about a quarter of the way from the start (**Figure 15**).

17. Reach through the tube, grab the other end, and pull it into the tube until you can match the remaining raw edges. You'll have a half-length tube with right sides together. Stitch around the raw edges (**Figure 16**). Use the gap left in the long seam to turn the tube right sides out.

18. Hand-stitch the gap in the seam closed (**Figure 17**).

19. Press the loop so that the long seam runs around the inside center.

20. The short seam allowance is the center back. Fold the loop to mark the center front. Baste and gather the short seam allowance and the center front (**Figure 18**).

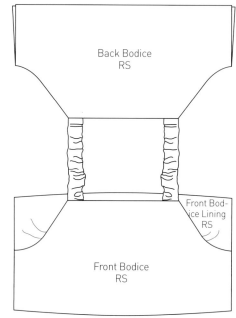

Figure 12

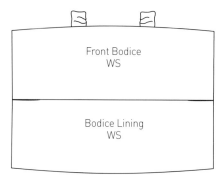

Figure 13

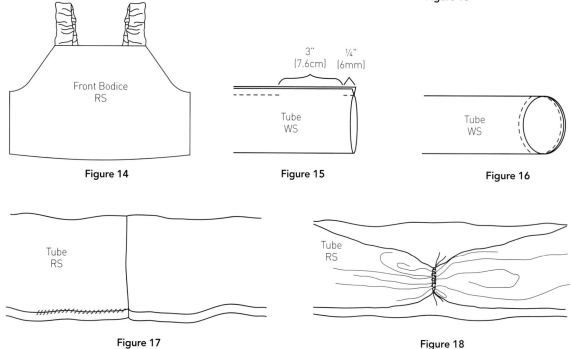

Figure 14

Figure 15

Figure 16

Figure 17

Figure 18

21. Stitch the shoulder loop to the center front and center back of the bodice (**Figure 19**). If desired, hand-stitch a large decorative button or flower over the gathers (**Figure 20**). Note that using a flower may make the dress not machine-washable.

22. Fold the overskirt panel right sides together, matching the short edges. Cut a curve through both layers along the short raw edge that starts about 6" (15.2cm) in from the edge and about 7" (17.8cm) up the side (**Figure 21**).

23. Press the side curved and bottom edges of the overskirt ¼" (6mm) to the wrong side twice to form a narrow hem. Pin the narrower lace all along this edge on the wrong side; topstitch lace in place, securing the hem at the same time (**Figure 22**).

24. Fold the skirt right sides together, matching the short edges. Stitch the short edges; finish this seam. Turn one raw edge ¼" (6mm) to the wrong side twice, forming a narrow hem. Stitch the hem.

25. Turn the skirt right-side out. Sew the wider lace into a loop to match the loop of the skirt. Pin the wider lace to the outside of the hem edge of the skirt and stitch in place (**Figure 23**).

26. The skirt seam is the center back. Fold the skirt to mark the center front. Place the skirt inside the overskirt, with both skirts right side out, matching top edges. Gather the top edges to match the width of the bodice at the waistline; basting stitches for gathering should be sewn through both layers at the same time (**Figure 24**).

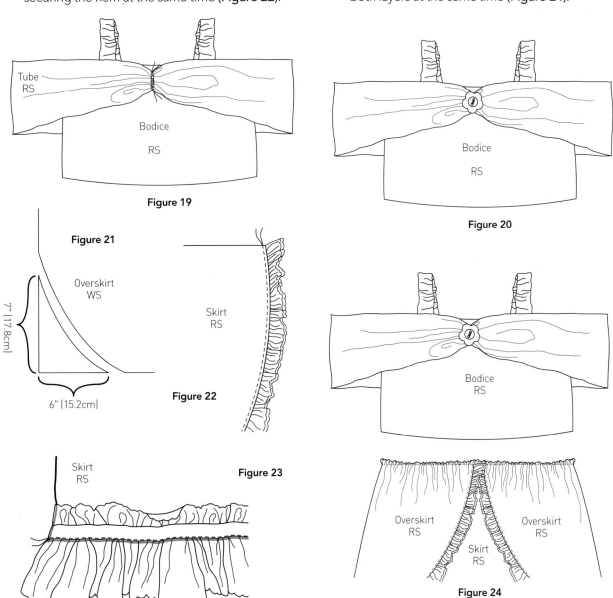

Figure 19

Figure 20

Figure 21

Figure 22

Figure 23

Figure 24

27. Turn the bodice lining side out. Press the bottom edge of the lining ⅜" (1cm) in to the wrong side.

28. Put the skirt/overskirt combo inside the bodice, matching waistlines, center back and center front. Pin the bodice outer fabric to the skirt combo and stitch through all three layers (**Figure 25**).

29. Pin the folded edge of the lining over the waistline seam. On the right side of the dress, stitch in the ditch of the waistline seam to secure the lining, or secure with a slipstitch (**Figure 26**).

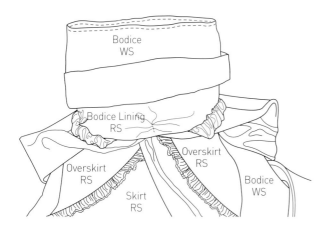

Figure 25

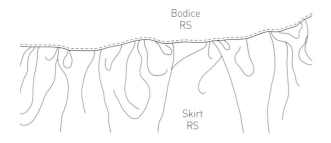

Figure 26

About the Author

Melissa Mora is the designer and owner of Blank Slate Patterns (blankslatepatterns.com) and the voice behind the popular sewing blog *Melly Sews* (mellysews.com). She spent twelve years in the classroom as a high school theater teacher before leaving to work full-time designing and writing for the sewing community. She now claims the entire Internet as her classroom and is on a mission to teach everyone how to make the clothes of their dreams for themselves and their families.

A native Texan, Melissa creates in Austin with her husband and two boys. Melissa can be found on Facebook, Instagram and Pinterest under Melly Sews.

About the Photographer

Alison Eden Copeland is an award-winning family photographer and rocking bass player. Her work has been featured in magazines as well as on several apparel websites and numerous album covers. She plays and shoots in Austin, Texas, with her husband, two boys, two roommates, two cats and one adorable dog. Alison does not sleep. Visit her online at alisoneden.com.

dedication

This book is dedicated to my mom, who taught me to sew, and to my husband and kids, who give me time to do it.

acknowledgments

I am so lucky to have supportive family all around me, and so they are the first people I need to thank.

To my husband, Kevin: You are my partner and my rock, and none of this would have been possible without you. Thank you for keeping me fed and saying yes to all my crazy schemes. I love you.

To my kids: Thank you so much for breaking me open and leading me to dreams I didn't know I had. I hope I will be as supportive of your dreams, and I can't wait to see you grow into them.

To my mom: You taught me to sew and connected me to your mother through that thread, and then got behind me to help me fly. Thank you, I love you, and I hope I've made you proud.

To my sisters-in-law, Heather and Jennifer: My brothers may have been a pain growing up, but they did good in picking the sisters they gave me. Thank you for always being willing to help.

To the rest of our family, especially Dad, Eddie, Jason, Jerry and Mary: You're always willing to step in and help, and that's just one of the reasons we love all of you. I'm glad you're never more than a text or phone call away.

Thank you to Alison, who helped realize my vision for this book and dealt calmly with crazy emails, last-minute scheduling and other minor crises. Your photographs are beautiful and I'm so honored to work with you.

Thank you to all the girls and women who appear in this book and enthusiastically supported my vision of showing a spectrum of womanhood in sundresses, from toddler to grandmother. Autumn, Tessa, Lindsay, Jaden, Lucy, Francesca, Stevie, Jada, Summer, Jessi, Ashley, Katherine and Yesenia, your inner beauty shines through. And thanks to the moms and families that brought these lovely girls and ladies to fittings and photo shoots and helped bring out their best on camera.

I have been fortunate on this journey to find a community of like-minded bloggers and designers. Designing and writing can be lonely occupations, and I am thankful for social media that keeps my "coworkers" close, though we are spread across the globe. These women have been invaluable supporters, mentors, business partners, cheerleaders, conference roommates and, ultimately, friends. Someday we should all live in a tiny house village with a great big central sewing room.

Thank you to everyone at F+W Media, especially Amelia and Noel. It has been a pleasure, and I couldn't have asked for a better first book experience.

Thank you to my sewing machine sponsor, Baby Lock. All the garments in this book were sewn on my Baby Lock machines (Elizabeth and Imagine). I am so fortunate to work with such an incredible company for the love of sewing.

Thank you to the fabric companies that sent fabric for some of these dresses—Sisboom/Jennifer Paganelli (sisboom.com), and Dear Stella (dearstelladesign.com).

Thanks to the Austin eateries that let us shoot on their property—Tamale House, Blue Dahlia Bistro and Hillside Farmacy.

And thank you to the readers and fans of *Melly Sews* and Blank Slate Patterns. Your encouragement and creations with my patterns and tutorials are why I love doing this. I can't wait to see what you do with the designs in this book—I was thinking of all of you as I wrote it.

a content + ecommerce company

www.fwcommunity.com

20   19   18   17   16   5   4   3   2   1

Distributed in Canada by Fraser Direct
100 Armstrong Avenue
Georgetown, ON, Canada L7G 5S4
Tel: (905) 877-4411

Distributed in the U.K. and Europe by
F&W MEDIA INTERNATIONAL
Brunel House, Newton Abbot, Devon, TQ12 4PU, England
Tel: (+44) 1626 323200, Fax: (+44) 1626 323319
E-mail: enquiries@fwmedia.com

Distributed in Australia by Capricorn Link
P.O. Box 704, S. Windsor NSW, 2756 Australia
Tel: (02) 4560 1600, Fax: (02) 4577 5288
E-mail: books@capricornlink.com.au

SRN: T7994
ISBN-13: 978-1-4402-4454-4

Edited by Stefanie Laufersweiler
Designed by Katherine Jackson
Layout by Karla Baker
Production coordinated by Bryan Davidson
Photography by Alison Eden
Illustrations by Sue A. Friend

We make every effort to insure the accuracy of our books. If an error has occurred, errata can be found at www.sewingdaily.com/errata.

Metric Conversion Chart

TO CONVERT	TO	MULTIPLY BY
Inches	Centimeters	2.54
Centimeters	Inches	0.4
Feet	Centimeters	30.5
Centimeters	Feet	0.03
Yards	Meters	0.9
Meters	Yards	1.1

Projects have been designed and created using imperial measurements and, although metric measurements have been provided, it is important to use either imperial or metric throughout as discrepancies can occur.

index

Dresses, for girls
    Bailey, 93–97
    Balcones, 39–41
    Bellevue, 111–115
    Driskill, 125–129
    Lady Bird, 149–154
    Littlefield, 71–75
    Metropolitan, 55–57
    Oasis, 137–140
    Palmer, 49–51
    Rosedale, 143
    Tarrytown, 105–109
Dresses, for women
    Fairlane, 77–82
    Mayfield, 131–135
    Olive, 43–47
    Parlin, 65–68
    Pennybacker, 87–91
    Primrose, 27–31
    Saltillo, 119–123
    SoCo, 59–63
    Sutton, 99–103
    West Lynn, 33–37

Fabrics, 10
    cotton broadcloth, 65
    cotton eyelet, 43
    cotton gauze, 49, 99
    cotton pique, 65
    cotton (quilting weight), 39, 55, 93, 105
    cotton twill, 71
    cotton voile, 131, 143
    dotted Swiss, 87
    nylon mesh knit, 77, 111
    nylon tulle, 125
    polyester charmeuse, 59, 119
    polyester chiffon, 119
    polyester georgette, 59
    polyester matte jersey (lining), 77, 111
    polyester satin, 125
    silk/cotton blend, 27, 33, 137, 149

Gathering fabric, 12

Measurements, 16–18
    adjusting bodice pattern, 18–20
    checking fit with a muslin pattern, 21
    dress measurement guides, 19
    skirt measurement guides, 23

Notions, 10

Overlock stitch, 13
    faux, 13

Rolled hem, 15

Seams, finishing, 13
    flat felled, 14
    French, 14
    overlocked, 13
Shirring, 12
Slip stitch, 15
Skirts
    circle, 22
    gathered, 22
    measurement guides, 23

Tools, 10

Zippers, 11

For More Adventures in Sewing

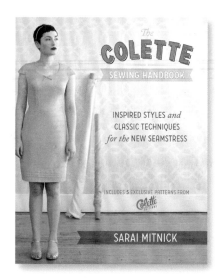

The Collette Sewing Handbook
Sarai Mitnick
978-1-4402-1545-2
$29.99

Sarai Mitnick is the pattern designer to watch. Her line, Colette Patterns, is quickly gaining popularity not only for its beautiful, nostalgic designs, but also for their ease of use and thorough instruction. In this book she shares the 5 fundamentals to the perfect sewing project, and offers 5 gorgeous projects, complete with tissue paper patterns.

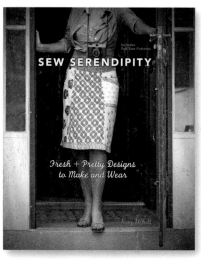

Sew Serendipity
Kay Whitt
978-1-4402-0357-2
$27.99

It's not a trade secret to alter a pattern to fit your figure and style—anyone can do it! Kay Whitt proves it in this gentle guide to clothes-making. Friendly math, solid coaching on how to measure for the best individual fit, and an overview of all the required sewing techniques ensures that readers will be on their way to making a coordinated, customized wardrobe.

BurdaStyle Modern Sewing: Wardrobe Essentials
BurdaStyle Magazine
978-1-62033-912-1
$29.99

Sewists know the BurdaStyle name and its reputation for high-quality fashion patterns. This collection from the archives of BurdaStyle magazine covers all of the must-have basics of a modern woman's wardrobe: jackets, pants, blouses, skirts and dresses. A Burda 101 section covers everything you need to know to follow the patterns.

For more great books, magazines and projects, visit www.shopfonsandporter.com